The Exodus of Being

Reflections on a Shipwrecked Life

The Exodus of Being

Reflections on a Shipwrecked Life

Saitya Brata Das
Isha Yadav

AAKAR

The Exodus of Being: Reflections on A Shipwrecked Life
Saitya Brata Das and Isha Yadav

First Published 2017

ISBN 978-93-5002-530-7

The publication of this book financially benefits from the University Grants Commission under the Special Assistance Program (SAP) that is granted to the Centre for English Studies, Jawaharlal Nehru University.

Published by
AAKAR BOOKS
28 E Pocket IV, Mayur Vihar Phase I
Delhi 110 091, India
aakarbooks@gmail.com
www.aakarbooks.com

Designed by
Limited Colors, Delhi 110 092

Printed at
Saurabh Printers Pvt. Ltd., Greater Noida

For
Those who are shipwrecked

To speak is to risk one's own existence, and yet, it is also the movement beyond by traversing the realm of death.

He who does not speak knows no hope, for hope is the venturing beyond into the unknown.

Contents

Prologue

I.

What follows is something like what the philosopher Theodor Adorno would conceive of a 'melancholy science': a 'minima moralia' for a shipwrecked life. Here reflections don't constitute themselves in the form of a system; in other words, reflections no longer *reflect* the identical, the immanent plane of continuum guaranteed by the self-presence of the Subject. What at best is possible is only a constellation or configuration without *Hypokeimenon,* a mosaic of aphorisms.

We no longer dare to provide maxims—pure forms of universality—that can be filled up with specific acts, or from which specific acts can be deduced. This can either be an occasion of despair or joy; this can also be an occasion to seize the lightning flash of beatitude liberated from constrains of the *arché.* Having to undergo a shipwrecked life and surviving it can truly be an-archic life, life given to the perils of the sea and to its demonic weather, without certitude: living like a rose—as Meister Eckhart would say—without a 'why', without the principle and without *arché.* The sudden arrival of beatitude, out of the abyss of the dazzling night, can even be a blessing, and can give us *life as life,* not the fragile beauty untouched by death but a life that has meanwhile passed through mortification and received it back redeemed. We don't have to think this peril of temporality as a dialectical passage that continuously gives us back the identical and the necessary. What we need to think is the radical contingency of the event that gives us, without necessity, the possibility and actuality of the wholly otherwise.

II.

Like my other book ....*And the World Should Be Made a Desert*, this book is also collaboration with an artist. Isha and I reflected together, and brought together, and yet each on his or her own manner—her images and my aphorisms—of what welcomes the lightning flashes of beatitude to a shipwrecked life, and what redeems it, without submitting the idea of redemption to the necessary logic of a determinate law. Whether the book says anything of that sort, it is for the readers to determine. We have taken the risk, that's all!

The Wound of the Absolute

1. The gift of being

To thank is to always thank someone for something given, but how to thank for being able to receive at all the very gift of being? Or, what does it mean to thank for being given this 'myself' (the receiver) at all, on the basis of which alone it is possible to thank someone for something (to receive something from someone)?

This is St. Augustine's question.

For me to be able to receive a gift at all, and to give thanks for the gift, I myself have always already been given (to me)—as if in a time before time, in a time before memory, the immemorial—that precedes any other gift ('this' or 'that' gift). Hence, this gift of the self which receives gifts is the more originary, and yet, precisely for that matter, is the immemorial par excellence; I can't trace it back to an 'origin': it opens me to the abyss which can only be responded by the abyss of love. What does it, then, mean to love God (this strange love which is the love of God!)?: to love with the love where the very possibility of loving is given to me beforehand, immemorially. I love God who himself gives me this very possibility of a self, and this very possibility of loving, who is thus more intimate than I am to myself! In the intimacy of 'me' to 'myself', *there* the gift opens an abyss of distance which is the very source of my being, where the gift separates me from possessing myself on my own ground. To love God, then, is to love with God's own love: therefore, it can only be a response, in the sense of *re-ponse*: it is not that I have love (that I possess love) therefore I (give) love (to the other); to love is, rather, to love without possession (to give without having, that means, impossibly). Love so dispossesses me that it opens an abyss for me!

One day I want to write something on St. Augustine, whom I love!

2. The wound of the absolute

The absolute that I desire—this alone do I desire in all my desires—has never stopped humiliating me each new day in the most beautiful and noble manner: on each new day being wounded by the absolute! In encountering the absolute (of truth or beauty), all the wealth that I have—the richness of my inner being and the richness of my outer existence, the fruits and the harvest that I have cultivated throughout my life (through education and through existential experiences to establish myself as this inner man in isolation, and in the external world holding this position among positions of social existence with other human beings)—comes to be nothing: all these resources debase or devalue themselves, as though I myself have to be reduced to the nothing to receive the wound of the absolute.

The absolute arrives to me like the wound of love, a divine wound that seeks to redeem me violently from the violence of the world. All I desire today is to open myself without reserve—this wound of my soul—to this excess that is paradoxical to the extreme, for the fullness of this event is simultaneously the utterly exposed naked being of mine.

3. The naked joy

Sometimes small things of our ordinary life give us indescribable joy: driving alone in a lonely, open road at night; sudden drops of rain on your skin; on returning home to find your child waiting at the gate for you; in the middle of a sleepless night, standing near the door of your bedroom, to hear the gentle breathing of your beloved people, and the joy that they have come to your life; momentary glances of a beautiful bird never seen before that perches in a tree of your garden, etc. The most authentic moment of joy in our life may exist in the most ordinary manner, in bare simplicity, in being able to accept the gift of one's existence, and in being aware that one exists at all without having to worry for what purpose, for what reason, or for what end: the bare, naked life in its pure simplicity can be an extraordinary joy!

I desire a purity which only saints or prophets appear to have. As a result, I almost always appear to live in a deficient mode of being. But, then, now and then there indeed occurs the gift of moments where purity happens, even though momentarily like a flash of lightning, as the event of truth (which is the very truth of my existence): in the naked simplicity of life, or, at the heart of my world there hollows out a movement of opening to a love and a beauty so absolute that tears alone can express, a joy not of this world! A beautiful lightness of being, ethereal and ineffable: everything suddenly looks simple and lucid, even the enigma of my own being, in the unfathomable abyss of a light. The language of this crystalline purity is the language of prayer.

When the world today devotes every day to the hedonistic consumption and instant gratification of pleasures which, once fulfilled, leaves us exposed to the absolute vacuity of our inner being to the point of despair, and where narcissism is the sovereign principle of world-hegemony, I think sanctification of life in the simplicity of joy- in the most old-fashioned way—as the only task worth taking: by an incessant work of love one must learn to abandon worldly attributes, and encounter being in the pure simplicity of its existence.

4. This torment of writing

So much goes on into the writing of a book if you are writing a book worthy of serious reading and thinking, such straining of your inner person. First of all, there is this endless battle with oneself where one fights with oneself to life and death; this despair to the point of abandoning the project so many times, and then again and again coming back to take it up; and this ecstasy of having suddenly and fortuitously to come across, after abandoning the project in total despair, this amazing formulation that you could never have imagined (if you would not have despaired). I am growing more experienced of writing books as I am growing intellectually–spiritually, but when I start with a new book, all these experiences really don't help much: I have to begin anew, from the very foundation of life, from the very beginning, and this same process, frightening and overwhelming at times, begins anew: despair, abandonment and incommunicable suffering, but also ecstasy and freedom, opening of a new horizon and beginning of a new metamorphosis of oneself. Many times, I still keep on writing and working while despairing over it all the same, because the growing of the book is so fascinating: as if the book gradually acquires to have its own life, and I am reduced only to being a signboard or maybe its caretaker; from this time on, as the book passes through me like a 'thorn in the flesh' (St. Paul) or like the sword of the spirit, I am deprived of the freedom—to abandon the book. The book, then, becomes a total obsession: it takes hold of me in a dream, or while awake with an obsession I cannot renounce. Then the impossible happens: I start writing at an imperceptible moment, as if the moment automatically happens, and then I look at it—lo!—I am completely astonished: 'what? Is it me who has written this? Is this hand that holds the pen through which the labyrinthine movement of writing is released, as if opening to the infinity, is this hand "mine"?' As if being dispossessed of all that "I am" and that "I could be", this abandonment of me to the empty desert of time, this itself which we call "writing", calls forth from me a responsibility that I cannot disobey: it is impossible to convey in language to others how traumatic this writing can be—which I undergo all the time, in my mind or on paper—a madness, a foolishness, a stupidity of some sort, an undertaking without any guarantee whether I will be able to complete the book. This trauma is also the moment of intense concentration, of immersion and absorption that, like an incessant movement, keeps carrying me on and on to the point when, on its own account, it decides to stop me: 'stop, Satya, this much!'

As I am thinking of undertaking more essential books, only the essential ones that I will write—even if I will write just one more book before my death—I am, frankly, terrified to extremity: writing a book is frightening, overwhelming, terrifying; but, you see, I don't have freedom not to write: I must accept, over and over again, this demand of writing, even though it involves despair or depression, this cursed existence of being an insomniac. When I see people blessedly asleep, I think to be able to sleep is the most blessed condition available to mankind; and only I am this accursed, tormented person, possessed by a ghost that I will never be able to conjure away.

I want to sleep one day. It will be such blessed sleep that I will never wake up again! In the eternal darkness, I will give up the light of my life: but then, the light will itself become so excessive and dazzling that it will be at one with this eternal darkness!

5. The lucidity of madness

People often think of madness as the confused state of mind. However, I know somehow intimately—and it is difficult speak of it—that in (certain) madness may there lie the highest lucidity and greatest clarity. The moments when I have come to the highest lucidity of existence, are those moments that often people call "madness".

6. Melancholy and violence

What frightens me most is the demonic that exists within me: there is in me certain energy or strength, a force or a power that can hurt others, or can even turn violent against others. Not only the actuality of being violent (and I may become violent on occasions), but the very thought that it is possible for me to be violent at all (even if it is not more than saying a strong word or saying something in a strong manner, in anger for example)—this very possibility within me—makes me infinitely melancholic, especially if the other person happens to be weaker than me (physically or socially): once I utter such a strong word, and happen to look at the other's face—who is bewildered and crushed—my whole inner being melts into despair. I am always shocked to see people—people who can be so near to us in our everyday life, people who can be our friends or colleagues—who can suddenly say something unspeakable and painful to us without feeling even the slightest bit of remorse or sadness: it is this inhumanity in human beings, which is so pervasive in our daily life in the most banal way, that I find most cruel and painful. It is this inner fascist within me that I am most scared of: this is what is the most demonic and terrible within me.

7. The extraordinary wound

What is exceptional can also be at the same the most ordinary. Since the exceptional hides itself in the proximate manner, we must often tear it—in a creative violence—from the many layers of oblivion that constitutes our quotidian life. This is why what is the most ordinary is not thereby easiest: it is often a most unbearable and painful wound. A tragic relationship, and yet extraordinary in the ordinary way: like our relation to death, or memory of a lost love!

8. The wound of the inexpressible

It is nearly impossible for me to write a critical response to a poem or to a work of art. A painting fascinates me, I am drawn to it as one is drawn irresistibly to one's beloved; a beautiful musical piece evokes a thousand nameless emotions of my buried life; a beautiful dance frees my body from the force of gravity; a sculpture makes me wonder how stones too cry out; and I weep like a child when in a play or in a film profound human experience is portrayed by a great actor. But to give a critical response to it: I am dumb, my tongue gets stuck somewhere, and my lips are sealed by the inexpressible. While momentarily opening my buried life to an overwhelming expression, once that is over, this work of art one again retreats into its closure, and I cannot translate it anymore into the language of sober prose. Quite early in my student years I realized this: that I cannot be a 'literary critic' or 'cultural critic': it is just hopelessly difficult for me! This business of 'literary' or 'cultural' criticism, admirable though it is, is not for me; I gave it up, fortunately so.

The work of art, however, has continued to fascinate me, especially painting. Now I approach a work of art, while enjoying it, as if from an irreducible distance, going around-about- way, saying-without-saying: this is the reason why in my writings I do not talk much about works of art (while teaching in literature Departments). A hesitation, a certain withdrawal, and a certain looking-away-while-look-at: not because I don't think highly of literature or work of art, but precisely the other way, as if there is something that I don't want to say, that something I cannot speak, and I don't know what is it that is so secret, so enigmatic, so much a riddle!

9. The pilgrim on the earth

Outwardly my life appears to have "everything", lacking nothing: family and friends, positions and success; but what I lack is precisely the essential and decisive for me: the idea in which the infinite comes, the infinite idea. For (most) others "everything" comes first and the idea come last, if at all it comes to them; for me, the idea is the first priority and "everything" comes later. That is to say: I exist "upside-down": what for others is a blessing is for me a curse, and vice-versa. While most people live horizontally, I live vertically, that is: from the summit having to look down at the yawning abyss, or, from the abyss having to look up to the dizzying height.

It is extremely difficult to convey the world (so far I have not been successful with regard to a single individual) that I have a different experience of pain, and a different conception of joy; that I live differently inwardly while externally I live just like any others. But the truth is that I don't share this world with anyone, not because I live for myself alone (in a narcissistic manner), but that I am a stranger to the world, an eternal pilgrim on the earth. What I share, in the true sense of the term, is not the worldly world but immortality.

What, then, makes me singular is that I hold together, at the same instance, the absolutely heterogeneous elements—inner and outer. What for others is an inhospitable abyss of contradiction is for me a daily bread for nourishment. Only recently I am intimated with the infinite idea—hardly known to most people around me—that: what perils us is also what redeems us.

10. The wound of silence

It is now the time of silence, the great night of silence in whose depth the essential word is to prepare for itself its own birth. The word, coming out of the womb of the night, bears within itself the enigma of the night and it is a singular intrigue of creation: how within the transparency of the light, which the word has come to be now, there still lies the mystery of darkness, like the rudimentary memory of some immemorial past!

All essential word, each one of them being singular and unique, has the wound of the silence within it, in the same way that—to speak in the language of dialogue—silence is pregnant with the speaking word. This is why the poetic, or, the philosophical word, which always carries the memory of creation in it, appears so mysterious in its very fecundity: we must learn silence so as to speak; but the reverse is true too: we must learn to speak so that silence comes to us, silence which is not the negation of speech but it's beatific fulfilment. This is why our profound happiness is so serene, even silent: it is the moment when language attains its Sabbath, which is the seventh day of the week, the day of rest, and which, precisely thereby is the holy day , the day that is holy, the day when the whole week is sanctified and consummated.

It is now for me the time of night, and at night to prepare for the word to come: long is the night, but if it is well spent, how glorious will be the day! Come to me, oh the abyss, so that the word transfigures you into the eternal light, so that I may pass into eternity through the great gateway of the dawn!

11. The veil of melancholy

I must no longer try running away from this irreducible veil of melancholy through works but, giving a pause to writing, I must now decisively confront the abyss of my being by an inward deepening. What is necessary now is less writing and producing but that of an existential transformation through the plunge into the unfathomable depth of my own existence, opening to that invisible spring of all life where everything becomes stillness and silent.

There seems to be residing something within me so unfathomable that I always seem to remain outside its gate and I don't have the key to it!: a secret even from myself, beyond memory and knowledge, and yet which is the very central fire of my inner being that invisibly moves all that I feel, think, sense: a memory before memory, a language before language—an immemorial language that haunts, in an eternally mournful tune, the secret depth of myself.

I now need to talk to myself more than ever before, and more than with anyone—in utter solitude, deeper than anything else that I have ever known. And I must talk in a language which is nourished by overflowing silence of the elements—of the sky and the sea, of mountains and trees.

12. Grace

I am dedicating the essential task of my life—the only one thing needful—to God, for everything that I am blessed with: happiness, love, thought and my existence itself as gifts coming from Him alone. They are the rays from the fire of the sun that gives warmth and vitality, but also scorches us and burns us if we become arrogant enough to cross the limit of our mortality.

In a deeper sense, the limitation of our mortality is no limitation at all, but rather is the very wound that gives us life. It is only on the basis of our finitude can we be open to infinity; it is the measure of mortality that exposes us open to the bliss of the immeasurable.

Our mortality is not a cage of the law and fate, but the very possibility of freedom and happiness, and this freedom is the very ground of all that we mortals think, experience and do. It is true that this freedom can turn us into demons (which explains the possibility of radical evil: Schelling has something profound to say about this), but this is also the very condition of our being open to divinity and to our redemption.

Most of us don't know what to do with our lives and with ourselves. The task is to actualize this freedom in a measured way by regulating it to the establishment of justice and expression of love. When that happens, our life is fulfilled: we become like gods—happy, blessed, and blissful!

13. Purity alone matters

When human beings encounter the deepest abysses of loneliness, they respond basically either in one of the following ways: there are some who, staking their whole being in finite things or beings, endlessly run from one being/thing to another, endlessly dissatisfied in each thing in turn, yet knowing nothing else, torment their already wretched and lacerated consciousness, for each thing can be nothing other than only a substitution of another equally wretched thing, a mirror image of one's own laceration: this is the path of the libertine; then there is another, when the human being, by a singular manner of individuation, ethically and spiritually orients himself absolutely to the absolute through an essential work of life: this is the ethical or religious path.

Between these two paths, there are many attenuated variations of subterfuges: there are those who are basically libertines, but they disguise themselves under religious dress; these are the most despicable people on earth, and they are basically hypocrites; many of these people are called 'intellectuals', or, what nowadays they call themselves as 'spirituals'. Those spirituals who are intellectuals too, make their career by writing books on spirituality or by opening up spiritual institutions where thousands gather seeking consolations. In other words, they are basically making their capital out of the vulnerable mass of gullible people who are lacerating under the most inhumane condition of extreme capitalism. Many people in today's era of mass consumption throw themselves into this most malicious and devouring hunger where the wild beast disguises himself as the well-behaved, civilized man, while still hunting for the ever new prey. A self-confessed libertine, following the path of endless satisfaction that each time leaves him intoxicated, is—compared to all these spiritualists—is a far more admirable and respectable person; there is even a dignity about him, while the spirituals are downright despicable and pathetic.

Only purity saves us. Only purity, with which longing for the infinite rises from the depth of the abysses to the summit of heaven, may encounter the absolute which alone can match with and overcomes this central fire of emptiness in our inner life: for it is all love and all life, and its warmth does not devour us but nourishes us with serenity and blessedness.

14. Life is still empty!

There is a dreadful loneliness and utter emptiness at the centre of existence which no finite thing and finite being seems to fulfil; the void gnaws at the ground of being, and we, desperate, run like mad animals from one substitute to another substitute only to find each one of them dissatisfying. So life passes its course in a vicious course of endless substitutions, still hungry, still naked and still abandoned, till it reaches the brink of the abyss, the edge of the definitive fall. Even when the cup is brimful with the sparkling wine, life is still empty!

15. Without "why"

There is indeed something solitary about thinking, about a certain kind of thinking that we call 'philosophical': a serenity that does not rush along the movement of the world but tends to go slow, taking its own time, like the undulating waves of the pregnant sea, or like the blessed beauty, almost melancholic, of the autumnal landscape of the countryside. Nothing matters any more, but just like to be a rose or the lily in the field: 'without asking why' (Meister Eckhart).

16. Of loneliness

For most individuals loneliness and suffering have purely physical-social and psychological (or emotional) meaning, meaning that can be understood to bear more or less determinable situations and conditions. What appears to evade them is another kind of loneliness and suffering: an intellectual-spiritual loneliness and suffering. That something like the latter exists at all, and that it involves the entirety of one's being, and therefore can't be understood to be one kind of loneliness and suffering among others: this experience, which is irreducible to any given determination and cause, is incomprehensible, so much so that such is immediately fixed as 'elitist' or 'bourgeois' luxury!

For certain individuals all 'experiences' are to be transfigured—and thereby also be redeemed—into something intellectual and spiritual: all spiritual works that creative individuals take their birth from such a transfigured and redeemed suffering, as though as it were, all human suffering and joy, groaning and crying, longs for such transfiguration and redemption. That this is what may constitute something like a vocation for certain individuals, at the most profound and highest level, is incomprehensible, and it is often considered to be either a claim for aristocracy or downright stupidity!

17. Mournful joy

When life looks empty and desolate and 'all that solid (of life) melts into the air' (Marx), we often run around—like an animal stung by bees—looking for consolations in vain things: one looks for consolation in fleeting human relationships, tries to find a friend somewhere around, or to sink oneself in inessential entertainments that only momentarily leave us in oblivion only to let the ghost of desolation haunt us once more. And one knows nothing helps: one discovers one's friend recoiling and receding from her, and everything else vanishing like vapours into the thin air. The ground beneath our feet suddenly disappears, and lo, the Archimedean point is not to be found. How, then, should one not allow life to be sucked into the yawning abyss of desolation?

Only giving oneself, unconditionally, to one, and one only, vocation of life where one's whole existence can be poured into, and where one can put at stake one's entire being can help one transform the abyss of life into the very possibility of existence, and that vocation has to be indeed the unconditional one and must have an absolute meaning; while everything else floats away into the deluge of time, it must alone retain its absolute sense to which one must, with the strength and fragility of one's being, remain in fidelity. That means, inversely, one must renounce putting too much stake of one's life in the conditioned phenomena of the world; one must accept, gratefully, a kind gesture coming from one's friend in our desolate times, but one must not put a stake in it, and not expect from her as if she owed it to me: it is a gratuitous gift coming wholly uncalled, and I don't deserve it as your merit or by any debt! Similarly any consolation that comes from any destination of life, even from God: nobody owes me anything, and what comes, comes to me only as gratuitous and uncalled gift, which may only be hoped for but must never be demanded or claimed.

This realization is the most painful realization I ever had: not to ask anyone for anything, and to think everything in life, an event or a relationships, purely as a gift, and never as a value or a demand. But it is also liberating: nothing is more liberating than this in life, a liberation that comes only at the cost of great pain. This is why philosophy and religion are closer to life than anything else, for this existential teaching is the highest teaching of philosophy and religion: the mortification of the will, and renunciation of claim—upon oneself, upon others, and upon God! One must not ask for consolation, in our desolate time, even from God: he owes me nothing, absolutely nothing, and one must ask God absolutely nothing, apart from praying to him that I may be able to pray at all, and have faith in him! This leaves me with such a profound joy of which there is no worldly analogy: a divine joy, a serene joy, a joy tinged with a divine mourning.

18. *Askesis*

Our deep, profound joys come only with renunciation. The modern human being asks too much from himself, too much from the world and from God. We refuse to accept what is given to us, and instead run after chimeras and fantasies. Our world of extreme civilization of technological domination and calculability daily feeds each one of our erotic fantasies with the powers of virtuality and spectacle: we desire too much pleasure from our bodies, too much from our little hearts, too much from everything. This malicious hunger for fulfilment, from chimeras and fantasies, never ceases to daily abandon us to laceration and savagery. From the very early years of our life we are programmed (as in a machine) by our parents, our schools, the world around us, to achieve great success in the world and to accumulate an insane amount of money and materials, but what ultimately happens?: at the age of 35 or 40 a young man is already exhausted and has become decrepit like a 60 year old individual, a mere cog of an immense, anonymous, cruel apparatus—an inhuman, cold, technological piece!

It is good to practise a bit of renunciation every day, and look for true joy and happiness where it essentially lies: not in self-assertion and planetary domination in the godless world, but giving up daily a claim upon oneself, claim upon others, claim upon the world, and even claim upon God. In other words, as Meister Eckhart beautifully and heretically says (for which he was condemned as a 'heretic'): one must give up even God, and not just the world! 'Religion' (understood in this sense) is a great temptation in the technological world of world-historical domination: 'religion' and technology are two sides of the same coin—our desire of mastery, over God on one hand, and on the other hand, over the forces of nature and the human.

19. This fragile heart!

How fragile is this little heart of ours, and yet how prodigious love and pain may it suffer! This is why even God chooses to attack, with the arrow of his love, this fragile hut of our existence: he traumatizes us with his overflowing wine of love and does it such infinite violence! Who among the lovers can speak of how violent love can be?

20. Grace alone can save us

The evil forces possess a demonic energy and a fiery will in relation to which the good only appears so destitute and fragile. Everything seems to support the demonic force, while the good appears as if at the extreme limit of the world, a remnant that is only too disappearing, like the faint murmur of a muffled sigh!

How to survive this destruction of the good, of justice and truth? Where can one put faith in? Everywhere the eye turns the demonic forces are triumphant! As if only grace—the supernatural elevation of existence—can effect the transfiguration of the force of gravity that is constantly pulling us down to the abyss of the dark night.

This is the deepest melancholy of creaturely existence: it erupts from the violence of gravity which is the deepest tendency of being. Only a violence which must be such that it surpasses all violence emanating from gravity, such violence of grace alone can save us from this utter annihilation!

The Abyss of Crucifixion

1. A thorn in the flesh of the world

When I look back at the long way on which my life has run its course, I find my life incomprehensible and mysterious, as if a secret force whose name I don't know, has all the time been working on my destiny, a secret that refuses to yield to my knowledge, that enigmatic riddle which has never ceased to surprise me every now and then. It perhaps will not make sense to people if I say that I have always been surprised by myself; while trying to understand myself, I discover myself that I could not think that I can be what I am now. Born in a very humble family, with a father whose qualification is matriculation and my mother being just Class 8th pass, no one in the entire line of ancestors all through the generations even had an inkling of what I engage with (namely, philosophy); reading books in the dim light of those kerosene lamps (every evening I have to clean my glass lamp); selling milk of our cows on the way to my school in the morning and in the afternoon, after coming from school, cutting grass for the cows; surviving with one pair of sandals for years that I need to keep repairing in every second month (yet not telling my father, who has three more children apart from me, that my sandals are long time back worn out: at the age of 11 I was already 25 years old); saving 25 paisa every day from the money my parents give me for lunch so that I can buy for myself a book after 15 days; wearing my elder brother's leftover shirts by doing little bit change in it (they call it " altering"); playing with balls made of worn out wools and papers because we cannot buy a ball to play (oh, those infinite memories!); having the opportunity to make my first phone call when I was already in my Masters; using the lift for the first time when I was 22 years old (I used to tremble in fear); seeing trains for the first time when I came to my University in Delhi; we did not even have proper toilets at our home; walking kilometres just to watch a TV series on Sunday morning: could I imagine, then, that I would be a professor one day in the country's best university; that I would read Hegel—one of the greatest philosophers of all time—for my PhD; that I would do post doc in Paris and Strasbourg; that I would publish from Edinburgh University Press and Oxford University Press; that I would have such a lovely child and a family; that I would one marry someone from Mumbai?

I never stood first in any class. Though quite intelligent (I did not know then that this adjective "intelligent" can at all be applied to me; still now I am not sure whether it is true or just a false compliment that people make out of pity for me) I was, but never "phenomenal" or even remarkable; there were better students in my school; I was surprised by myself, but vaguely and secretly I expected this, when I got a First Division in 10th exam; I was surprised when I went to read Shelley in my college (my first intellectual love!) that even I can read Shelley (what a beautiful name: Shelley!); what surprising joy that even I could read Nietzsche (my second intellectual love: he haunted me for 12 long years!); what an incredible thing that even I had the potential to get into JNU to study (perhaps the most important event in my life after my birth); what an astonishment to discover philosophy (I am just meant for philosophy; or philosophy is just meant for me?); how incredible a thing to discover that I am not the worst one among some of the best students in the country who come to this University! Is it me?: Whom those upper caste neighbours of my village used to laugh at for being a Dalit and call by those horrible names (dirty, stinking Dalit that I am!), whom they don't allow entry beyond their living room because I am a Dalit who contaminates everything he touches: is this me, this professor in JNU, this beloved scholar beyond the country? Am I the same person?

Behind me lies this immense history of suffering, of unshed tears, of muffled cries, of unuttered pain: how can I forget this? Yet when I look back at the long course of my life (such a long journey), I realise that suffering is essential to life, that suffering is the greatest gift that God gives to a human being, for through suffering alone we acquire the highest knowledge, the tragic knowledge of life (that is why Shakespeare's *King Lear* is my favourite play). My father, the first great teacher I have had, used to tell me this parable: when a tree, even though it is a great tree, bears too much fruits, it bows down; it does not haughtily erect its head! I took this best knowledge in my heart: I must be that tree who bears so many fruits that it must bow down in humility and gratitude!

Suffering is essential in life! Is not God himself who suffers? This is why I am Christian in spirit (I have not converted myself, I don't need to) who is born of Hindu parents: the God dying on the cross, his flesh torn out and his blood pouring out, his eyes are empty sockets: oh, this absolute abandonment, utter loneliness and absolute pain—yes, this God speaks to me! He seems to be just like me: a Dalit mocked and laughed at by the world, spit by the wise, a crown of thorns on his head! I am Christ! The Gods my parents worship don't speak to me: all of them, apart from one proletariat God (whom I like), no one of these gods knows suffering; they are too much high above; all of them are kings or Brahmins wearing diamonds and gold in their many hands, ruling over the cosmos, and yet knowing not even slight pain. Only with Buddha (who is not God in the sense that Vishnu is) that I can feel that tremendous and prodigious pain of human existence being embodied, who knew suffering—while being a prince!—and death, and knows that absolute moment of desolation of our human existence!

Looking back, I feel that despite sufferings—or, better, because of it—my life is beautiful! I am meant to have this life through which God weaves the destiny of my life in his invisible spinning wheel. For what he gives me, through suffering, the joy that truly liberates us from the iron wheel of fate. It is through me God himself suffers so that he will attain the highest joy. I must accept this God within me, and devote my whole intellectual, spiritual, physical energy to this single task of life, given to me by him, that God suffers through each mortal being , that in the suffering of the other person or any other being, God himself suffers on the cross! So we must suffer for another being—the other human being—it does not matter whether he is Indian or Pakistani, Hindu or Muslim, man or woman, rich or poor. I must allow this tragic wisdom to be expressed as the decisive expression of my philosophy, for this is what I am meant to do. If philosophy were only an academic subject, how useless would it be for me! So this God—the downtrodden, the most minus figure of history disfigured on the cross of the world, the Dalit or the most repressed one—keeps hidden the mystery of my life from myself so that unknowingly I may fulfil what I must, for which I am born for these few days on this earth so that finitude can be the very medium through which infinite may express itself as the very riddle of eternity!

It is good to be poor in knowledge so that through our foolishness the divine wisdom comes to us! All through my life, I am only training myself to be foolish, a scandal, a crown of thorns, and a thorn in the flesh of the world!

2. The persecuted truth

The truth of persecution is that what or who is persecuted—accused, accursed, mocked or laughed at, spat upon, condemned—is in truth, for truth is always persecuted. It bears on its head not a diadem of diamonds but a crown of thorns.

3. Hope against hope

From the history of mankind we learn one thing: that the greatest heroes of humanity are not the princes and emperors but martyrs, those fools who don't even understand the most simple worldly wisdom: that mankind can't be reformed; that what we describe as 'civilization' is but only a new form of barbarism; that behind the glorious pages of world history there lies, in invisible ink, countless sighs and muffled cries of the oppressed and vanquished.

Every genuine hero of humanity is a martyr—one who is spat upon, crucified, made to drink poison, excluded or banished from the human community, and abandoned to be killed by beasts of prey, without honor and burial.

This is the highest paradox of human history. The philosopher who looks at the tragic spectacle of history cannot but be—at certain moments—moved by a profound despair, but also by a strange hope, hope against hope, a hope closer to madness than to reason: that the world may be saved, if at all it will be saved, from catastrophe precisely by these fools, those most idiotic and useless people, these excluded and crucified ones, these who are spat upon, these ugly people born amidst the beautiful human race.

This is why the philosopher or the martyr—who by definition is the lover of beauty—is the most enigmatic sort of person, the chosen ones: being a fool, he is wise; being ugly he bears the most ravishing beauty and seduces the young; being excluded from the human community, they build up new foundations for *the community to come*; being crucified he redeems through suffering!

4. The cross of history

For many of us—those who are much educated in critical thinking—the idea of religion is a scandal and a folly; and for the more aristocratic of us who are even more trained in critical exercise of human reason, religion is either one of these—a myth or a dogma, an ideological boomerang, a mirage on the desert of false consciousness.

The religious turning of my thought—in a profound sense there is no "turning" at all—in other words, my more explicit grappling and struggling with the question of "religion" (where the very idea of "religion" itself is at stake, and thus not to be taken for granted and be presupposed in entirely restricted and constricted senses of "myth", "superstition", "dogma" , or even as an inferior level of truth, etc.), has provoked and evoked sneers, laughter, criticisms and even downright dismissals of me by my very intellectual peers and friends: somehow there is a suspicion that I may have abandoned my previous "radical" (whatever that means; whatever they mean they mean in a "good" sense, however) viewpoints; I may have become more "conservative" or "orthodox", or one of those "spiritual seekers" (which has become a multinational industry these days: the commodification of religion has never reached such heights as these days!), or even just shifting my adherence from one religious institution to another, equally repressive apparatus (from Hinduism to Buddhism or Christianity, for example, as if I have converted in any simple sense of the term!; as if I need to choose among various possibilities as one chooses a shirt in the market place); I see my friends mocking me, silently and carefully (so as not to offend me: after all we are friends; only that I have gone astray), when they see a book by Meister Eckhart or St Augustine in my hand!

However, never have I felt such joy at the responses, always well-meant, by my dear friends and peers, even more than when they used to admire (they still do, I feel) my intellectual courage and my "radical" views (have I really changed any bit of it?): previously criticisms by my peers, even though well-meant, used to affect me negatively; somehow these days when criticisms are becoming more and even more "destructive" of me, I am even enjoying them even more, in the most child-like way (without envy and without resentment), and, the strangest thing of all, I don't even feel the necessity to defend myself. A peculiar calm is growing from inside, a sense of affirmation and security, and a movement of transcendence from the realm of intellectual justification and having to constantly defend oneself. What must religion be if not a "scandal" and a "folly"?: it is the truth inhospitable, and an indigestible remainder that murmurs away, like the faint cry of the oppressed, at the margins of the world! The truth of the cross is not the truth of the world!

I have remained at odds with the world (my favourite number is an odd number: 9, my birth date number!) in whatever I do: an eccentric in the family; at odds with the academic discipline where I am placed by luck; at odds with the world around me; and, above all, always at odds with myself! Religion, for me, must be at odds with the world and with the humanity as it exists today!: indigestible, offensive, stupidity, madness, scandal!

Here I am, with you and always without you, near you and always more distant than any one of you to others: I am indigestible, an offense, stupid and foolish, not completely "human" enough, a scandal on the cross of history.

5. Nietzsche and Kierkegaard

When one reads Nietzsche at one moment of one's life, especially early, and reads Kierkegaard at another moment, especially later, the result is tempestuous: one upheaval is followed by another, one quite contrary to the other, but also similar, precisely in their oppositions and precisely because of these oppositions. I don't know any other than these two—who are like polar opposites to each other—who shake the foundation of our existence to such radical manners, and abandon us exposed either to the yawning abyss below or the dizzying summit above. It then becomes then an immense task, an immensity that we can't even measure in thought or in knowledge, to re-establish the foundation of one's existence once more, if one is not to sink into the yawning abyss, or, to lose one's mind in the vertigo of the summit, for the tectonic slabs beneath our feet have meanwhile been shifted, and we are left with the void, either to leap over like it an expert dancer ,or to sink into it like wrecked ships in the bottomless waters of the sea.

Those moments of life when we need to arrive at the decisive decisions of life are the most radical events of one's life: everything else follows and are decided from these radical moments. And these radical moments begin with our exposure to the bottomless abyss of life. A human being is great to the measure that she confronts this abyss and by mortifications of her other petty wills, transforms gravity into grace and abyss to the summit, for—as Nietzsche says—the way to the summit is the same as the way to the abyss below.

We must seek greatness in life: not the greatness of the measureless accumulation of wealth or worldly success (name and fame), but the greatness of the spirit, giving up our intellectual and spiritual indulgence, and by engaging in works of truth or beauty. For what greatness of spirit is, is often invisible to the world, and in the daylight of history, so what is truly wisdom is like "folly" to the worldly wise, and what is truly beauty is like "scandal" (St. Paul) on earth. If we are to seek true beauty and truth, we must not be afraid of this folly and scandal: silently and quietly, like doves, we must keep on working towards our own greatness, bearing the cross, which is—as I said before—is not recognized by the world as "greatness".

6. The martyr and the slave

Whether a scholar is a true scholar or not, and whether he is worthy of our respect or not, must be judged, not by the parameter of how many books he has written, how many international connections he has, how many projects he has, etc., but by the following unconditional criterion: to what use he applied his knowledge (whether at servile use for petty worldly benefits, or, for the noble service of truth), and whether his works, even if they are few, have any transformative effect of our existence, and to what extend is he ready, for the sake of truth, to sacrifice his life. For, from the conception of truth, which must be the unconditional criterion, the martyrdom is an inseparable consequence.

Here is, then, the decisive criterion of true/false scholar: the false scholar is a slave to the world-political sovereign powers (he washes the hair and feet of princes), and the true scholar is a martyr: he is ready to sacrifice his life in the name of truth.

7. The absolute paradox of the cross

What I find most profitable these days is to withdraw, and to withdraw the stakes of one's whole existence from the world that is immediately given to us, a gesture that is close to what medieval mystics call "abandonment": neither the stoic *apatheia* nor what people generally call 'journey inward', but a deepening of inwardness that opens to the infinity of radical exteriority which, nevertheless, is not 'the world'! What is difficult to understand here is that there is something like an opening to an exteriority through inward deepening which exceeds the whole opposition between in the interiority of the presently given self/consciousness and exteriority of the presently given world.

The vulgar mysticism, as much as the worldly wisdom, is caught up in this opposition, and this is why it is not for nothing that the vulgar mystic at once presents himself to us as worldly wise. What interests me is rather something different: there is something like foolishness which is wiser than (worldly) wisdom! Who can understand, and who can bear this paradox?: unless he is ready to carry, at every moment of his existence, the cross of suffering!

8. The inhospitable remnant of the world

Only that which can now halt the world rushing towards its catastrophe is—religion. One can understand it only by thinking religion in its originary purity, and not in the garb of historical reason, for what presents itself today as religion, in our proximate manner, to our historical reason is nothing other than a purely political-secular institution, and hence is irreligious par excellence. Today, in our liberal-secular world, nothing presents itself as religion other than irreligion, and in that precise way, paradoxically, true religion can hope to retain, in its eschatological reserve, its original impulse: to remain a 'scandal and a folly' for the world; to remain incognito and absconditus; to remain inhospitable and indigestible remnant of the world.

9. Exodus of being

That one stands lonely and isolated among one's kinfolk and suffers exile in one's very land: this is the sign that he has been gripped and seized by a longing for something higher, something nobler that can be spoken only in a foreign tongue...

10. The earnestness of life

Only when we are exposed to the utter nothingness of our immediate existence in all its worldliness, in anguish and weariness beyond measure, only then is revealed the true earnestness of our life.

11. The face of the world

The deepest suffering of Christ on the cross is now the face of the world: the barren and starless sky at night, the deformed body hanging on the cross, those empty sockets that are his eyes, the one who is absolutely abandoned to the abyss of the desert while drops of blood keep trickling from his wounds, the descent into hell on Saturday by the one who is spat upon and given ignominious death while murderous cries of those murderers roar in the distance...

12. Crucifixion

Only in the figure of Christ dying on the cross, disfigured and abandoned, against the black, empty sky of the night that I find a reflection of my experience of the absolute abandonment, that ultimate loneliness in confronting the abyss of nothing where not only the world but God too abandons him on the cross. That is why, spiritually and existentially, I am so Christian: no other God is so abandoned as Christ! It refuses any worldly consolation; one who contemplates this disfigured figure enters into the utter desolation of the desert!

Without identifying myself with any denomination and any institution, and therefore without having to convert myself, I am profoundly Christian in spirit, in the following sense and understanding: existence is the cross! Only two more days for the glorious resurrection, but these two days appear to be an interminable agony in hell. But hell is not "anywhere", in the underworld: it is this world itself that is hell! Hell is the world!

13. Truth is the cross

Truth can't be bought and sold at a bargaining price. Truth is to be understood in unconditional and absolute term: it is the non-negotiable and non-relative Good. Therefore there can't be politics of truth, but all politics worthy of its name must be carried out in the name of truth. Truth is what is persecuted!

Truth is the cross! Neither she who has drawn profit from the cross nor he who persecutes knows the cross: both abandon the cross in their ways. The cross is not profitable; it is the way where our eyes become empty sockets and the light of the world gets extinguished!

When truth wounds, then "stones too cry out"! (Luke 19:40)

14. That justice does not belong to the world

To preserve certain dignity and nobility of character, it is good to happily sacrifice something: some worldly benefit and profit which one can get by licking the boots of the authority in place, or buttering his mouth...

I feel sad to see the demonic forces of injustice win, but also happy that I am not giving up the dignity and nobility of character. Is it not that in the world injustice almost always wins? As if justice does not belong to the world! As if to belong to the world only amounts to an injustice...

Politics of World-Nihilism

1. The integrative violence of the law

What we don't learn in the (Indian) University system is precisely the essential: individuation of language in which the new arrives as the singularizing event of thought and being. This has something to do with the deeper spiritual (or, the lack of it) ground of our historical existence: individuation has never appeared to be the fundamental problem, question or task of our thinking and being; instead, what the traditional thought-system encourages (which our Universities have perpetuated), and which is intensified to the most degenerate form under the regime of extreme capitalism, is that of thinking and existing under the species that determines, in advance, of all our politics and ethics, of our being and acting. In other words, what triumphs here is the integrative violence of the law which, even in the 'space' called 'University', has never been considered a matter worthy of thought. While our intellectuals constantly put into question, and rightly so, the restriction or constriction of the University life (by political regimes or under economic hegemonies), they don't understand that these (the massive fund cut to UGC under the current political regime, privatization of education, instrumental rationalization of knowledge production, etc.) themselves are only symptoms of a deeper malady which has never become an affair of thinking out of the historical ground of our existence: the integrative violence of the law that subsumes every singularity under the force of the universal. Take the example of our affective-family life, take the example of our national-political life, or take the example of our ethico-cultural modes of being as they are embodied in all possible institutions of our historical existence: you will see only the genus or species exists, and each one of us is forced to be a mere illustration or deduction of these theorems (to put to use a mathematical formula). It is this metaphysical violence which constitutes the conceptual structure of our thinking and acting that is forever perpetuated by our institutions of higher learning.

Therefore, the complaint of our President that none of the Indian Universities figures among top Universities in the world (which is echoed today by the thoughtless mass of people, driving by a blind and dumb ideology, when they complain that the University people—scholars and teachers and researchers—are wasting the precious tax-payers' money: this has now led to a massive cut of funds to UGC by this current regime) is a completely myopic diagnosis (in fact it is not even a diagnosis): in fact, this in itself is a symptom of the sickness that has infected the very foundational ground of our historical-national life. Instead, to remedy what they diagnose as the problem—and which in itself is a further intensified symptom of the said disease—the national-political life of this country is gearing towards, in an unprecedented manner, to extreme technological progress and economic accumulation of wealth (both at private and national level): we are buying a huge illusion here which has such immense consequences that whatever possibility has remained of curing ourselves, has now been finished off absolutely. What is triumphing here again is: the integrative violence of the law!

2. Totalitarianism of politics

The immense political passion that consumes the Indian psyche is a thing both very good and quite not so good. On one hand, when there increasingly is taking place what we call 'depoliticization' or 'neutralization of politics' around the globe under the sovereign regime of capital mass consumption, it is a good thing that 'politics'—understood as critical reflection on the given condition as much as readiness to transform the given condition—should remain at work. Politics for Indian 'people' is the only absolute passion: everywhere everyone talks endlessly of politics. In fact, it is *the* religion in Indian society (joined together with Bollywood, Cricket, economy and mass media, it is an unfathomably vast apparatus) par excellence. On the other hand, this sovereign passion of politics is not really a good thing: we know nothing but only politics (politics by which I mean this vast apparatus: the parliamentary democracy along with all that goes with it today, joined with Bollywood, cricket, multinational companies and mass media); politics is total for us, an absolute presence, with no remainder outside of it. This totalization is alarming and dangerous: first of all, all possible human relationships are so completely defined on political terms that it is nearly impossible, for example, for a person who has a certain left leaning to be friendly with someone with conservative attitude. This immense Indian society is now divided by infinite divisions into infinite sects—along lines of religion, caste and infinitely complicated sub-castes and sub-castes of sub-castes, class, race, language, ethnic community, regional differences, political affiliations, etc—to such an extent that at any moment terrible violence may break into unspeakable force. For Indian politics which has no other understanding of politics than that of coming to form hegemonic force in turn (by murder or by duping), this vast empire of infinite divisions is an immense fertile soil that can be exploited and abused without end. This sovereign violence penetrates everywhere in all possible human relationships in Indian society that makes existing in this part of the globe an absolutely painful existence in everyday life: violence is the norm, a banal evil, and all human relationships are nothing other than oppressive negotiations with powers, forces, terrors.

What is less marked than the one just mentioned is the second: the near absence of anything truly 'cultural' modes of expression other than politics. Look at our newspapers, journals, books, films or anything you like, you will see only politics being discussed: there is literally no philosophy in India. The ancient Indian thoughts are so completely appropriated by self-proclaimed guardians of culture, who are mediocre at best, that it is nearly impossible to transform them into living tradition that liberates. The consequence of this is clear: lack of human sensitivity and human sensibility that pervades our everyday human existence in this part of the globe. One cannot imagine the horror that one feels when the most ordinary person whom one meets every day—who otherwise is so genial—the moment he opens his mouth and talks politics, the fascist is revealed in all its demonic expressions! We have today virtually no other culture apart from that which is sanctioned and favoured by Bollywood: theatre is withering away; classical music and dance have become exotic phenomena (our cultural theorists find this phenomenon liberating and emancipatory; I know scholars spending their entire lives counting kisses in Bollywood movies—which movie has the most number of kisses? they mean 'lip to lip kisses'!). This totalization of politics is oppressive. What exists in the name of politics in India is the immense politico-theological machine, an unfathomably immense regime of the law: life wholly permeated by the violence of the law, penetrated by conditioned negotiations of forces that reduce singularity of our existence into minuscule parts of the giant machine of political theology. But life, reduced to the law and to politics, is no life; it expires like foams or smoke into the vast anonymous sky, 'grey upon grey', of mere being alive.

I think, almost prophetically—it is too obvious for a keen eye to be prophetic about it—that this Indian society, wholly buying neo-liberal disease of economic well-being and vast accumulation of wealth, and at the same being hypocritically touchy about a glorious Indian spirituality, is rushing headlong to a catastrophe. Nothing is there any longer to restrain us from this disaster. We have given up everything that is even remotely beautiful and spiritually enabling: thinking and poetising, as Heidegger says, the only things that would have saved us from disaster; cultivating—in educational and religious institutions—of human sensibility and sensitivity that alone would have saved us from being civilized brutes; and above all religion—which has become in Indian society today either a purely political battle or intoxicating opium for people, a commodity to be sold—which would have posed for us the truly spiritual and existential questions of life: all this we have sold to the devil's advocate, and now the devil has come to take away on what he already has a claim.

Thus, what now appears to me to be absolutely imperative, is this: 'retreating the political'(to borrow this phrase from Jean Luc Nancy and Philippe Lacoue-Labarthe) in two fold senses of the term: to re-treat the political (to treat again, to deal with it again and anew, more radically than before), and retreat (from) the political, to realize that politics (as the conditioned realm of practical negotiation of forces and powers) cannot be the ultimate horizon of meaning for human existence and human social relations, and that other things exist—like ethics or religion that opens up, beyond the conditioned realm of politics, to the unconditionality of, let us say, love or responsibility, forgiveness or kindness. To withdraw from politics to think the political anew (mark that I have used two different words here: 'politics' and 'political'), which does not amount to give up politics but rather to think the political, opening it to the unconditionality of the ethical and religious.

3. Why I am not a Hindu

To make a confession: I never felt myself to be a Hindu! I don't recall hardly ever been inwardly moved by this religion in any form (whether the beauty of its liturgy or its icons, of its songs or its festivals) despite being profound religious person that I have been, apart from a few of those atheistic years of my student days. But I often remember having being moved (while attending Buddhist worship, or looking at the painting of Christ dying on the Cross, or Mother Mary holding her dead son on her lap) by Buddhism or Christianity, to the point of tears, to the point of inner conversion (not the institutional one): what is unique and decisive to Buddhism or Christianity—and this is the decisive thing—is the unbearable experience of suffering to the extreme point of the absolute, and there, at this absolute point zero, an absolute transfiguration of existence, calling forth from the abyss of suffering the possibility of universal redemption of humanity through grace, or the infinite compassion and unconditional offering of love, beyond all economy and beyond all conditions. From this I have come to think that this human suffering—this absolute suffering—what religion must be all about, for nothing moves my whole being—and I may pour myself wholly into this—is suffering, and the absolute demand from each one of us, to love the other person without conditions. There are two things that have so far stopped me from converting into either Buddhism or Christianity: 1. Afraid of hurting my mother; and 2. My intense awareness that any form of my total identification to any institutional-collective form of religion (or even any secular collective body, like the State or the linguistic community) will be disastrous for me. This crisis has been running through me, dividing my heart into two, all these years—but without solutions! Very recently, reading Simone Weil I have come to see this exact problem in her, and I feel completely like her when she remained outside the Church, while remaining Christian in the most profound spiritual sense of the term. This is also the same thing I find echoed in Søren Kierkegaard's qualitative distinction between Christianity and Christendom; and I find myself echoed in Ambedkar's—Ambedkar who was A Dalit—decisive break from Hinduism: I think I must now take the decisive break too, but without having to be institutionally converted to another religion. In that sense, my gesture is closer to Simone Weil than to Ambedkar, understanding at the same time the profundity of Ambedkar's thinking and acting: to create a new form of life, it must be a new Buddhism, a *religion to come*.

4. Politics of nihilation

Despair is the constant temptation for one who exists in the most abject and depraved condition; this is, in fact, what the dominants and victorious precisely want: that the Dalit must constantly be kept in despair so that no transformation of the given condition will be attempted. Despair is, in fact, the opium that the victorious masters constantly inject and intoxicate the downtrodden and the vanquished. There is, however, a truth about this: that this despair—unlike what the poets dream of when they write poetry about suffering at night, and during the day join the very repressive ideology—that this despair is real.

What we must learn is that despair, however naked and brutal it is, is never the absolute experience of humanity, and that it does not have to be the ultimate horizon of meaning for us. Beyond despair there exists the miracle of pure affirmation, the unconditional affirmation that transcends despair: forgiveness and love without conditions that alone can save us from being hurled into the abyss of annihilation. The movement that liberates—unleashed by the Dalit (by virtue of what Walter Benjamin calls 'weak messianic power')—is not meant for the Dalit alone: everyone, even the oppressor, must be redeemed from the cages of historical violence. Only such an ethics of pure affirmation, beyond the dialectical politics of mere opposition (ethics in relation to which politics at all may receive its significance): this alone can save us from being frozen into stones by despair and violence.

While nowadays, people talk of Dalit-politics, I prefer to talk of ethics (first) and politics (opened up by the former and in the name of the former). Therefore, even the word "Dalit" can only have the sense of "transition". When at the end of the world justice will be established, the Dalit will disappear; there will no longer be any more "Dalits".

To strive after such disappearance—to refer to Walter Benjamin—that is the ethics and politics of the repressed.

5. Spiritual life

The contemporary Indian society has not even the remotest sense of "spiritual life". When my European and American friends, weary of their own civilizations, come to extol the mystical glories of Indian spiritual life (thereby exotisizing India), I take pains to repress my laughter (there is within me such sardonic power that I have to constantly repress it because of its violence): they don't see that India has completely bought up the logic of planetary domination and the logic of neo-liberal economic theology. Our religious institutions, which are often visited—often in good faith—by these world-worn foreign friends, are corrupted and diseased to the deepest level, to such an extent that they cannot visit them without being exploited (I know many and many stories of how Europeans and Americans are exploited, sometimes even raped, in these institutions). Thus the whole (illogical) logic that our Indian academics offer and make their careers out of this absurdity, the logic of the opposition that Indians are spiritual, and Westerners are materialistic: this is a downright lie, a ruse or cunning to cheat people who are already intoxicated and depraved. What is worse is the consolation that is offered to the worldly worn civilized people in this and other parts of the world: the downright degenerate version of mystical hedonism, and this unholy alliance of mysticism and technology (what a sick combination!). Thus, the idea that (Hollywood movies are full of these fantasies, especially science fiction movies), the East has still kept in shelter the remnant of redemptive values for mankind: this is either complete ignorance or still another lie. (Most of) Our postcolonial and nativist scholars make their careers out of the claim that they have finally turned the table upside down. They thereby betray their supreme ignorance when they say that the West does not know anything "spiritual" (forgetting the still alive mystical traditions of millenniums old), while in truth there has always been in Europe an insistence of a radical spirituality, sometimes even heretical, that has never ceased to radically put into question the very foundation of our historical existence, even if—and this is true—this possibility is slowly withering away even in the West.

It should be a matter of thinking whether these geo-political categories themselves need examinations ("East" or "West"), for they are never neutral and innocent as they are supposed by both Indian nativist and post-colonialists: when they talk of "locality" (this is the obsession of English departments of India for many decades now), that only India-born theory is applicable to understand Indian reality, this is downright a pseudo-problem. They somehow presuppose, without questioning, that ideas/ concepts/thoughts follow the same logic that geographical territories follow. The most decisive thing here is as follows: there is nothing today for Indians to give themselves the belief that India is the new messianic power which will redeem the world rushing towards an apocalyptic catastrophe; far from it, India has joined with other super worldly powers in the destruction of humanity. We have no resources left to turn the clock back again.

6. Violence of Hinduism

While a preponderant mass of this part of the globe along with many other people from the rest of the world is suffering from Islamophobia, recognizing in this religion a violence (the concept of 'jihad' is actually a theological concept and means something else; it does not mean what the secular-political abuses make of it, whether by Islamic fundamentalists or by Islamophobic others); and while postcolonial nations, justly so, point out the violence that came with Christianity: 'with the Bible in one hand, and guns on the other'(but Christianity in its spirit is entirely something else: it is the suffering of divinity and humanity, and the story of the redemption of the world by renunciation of violence) ; and while today secularists-Marxists and religious people alike want to reduce the violence of Israel state into religious violence (as if the Jewish people are essentially violent; they forget that the Old Testament makes messianic violence irreducible to any profane political violence), there is hardly anything profoundly said about violence in Hinduism, as if there is no violence in Hinduism at all. I don't know anyone apart from Ambedkar—and a few here and there, but nobody at the same level and intensity—who seriously has ever engaged with this fundamental violence of Hinduism. Hinduism has always been, in letter and spirit, extremely violent: millenniums of history can be evoked as testimony and document of its barbaric violence. But the interesting point is that while Christianity has great heretics and in great numbers (all these great mystics like John of the Cross, Teresa of Avila, Meister Eckhart and Jacob Bohme were persecuted). While Christianity has great critiques of its own fundamental violence (in Kierkegaard and others), the heretics of Hinduism are reduced to silence and invisibility (for there must be also some heretics in Hinduism).

It is surprising that while religion is such a fundamental problem in this country, there have never been serious religious studies in India, apart from history or sociology of religion kind of study, or some spirituality seeking kind of things: religion has never been in India a part of its philosophical-theological scrutiny. This is the immense lack: we have not been able to investigate the fundamental presuppositions of this culture which is essentially religious in character. This is because of a deep-seated anxiety: we are afraid to encounter the deep seated and unconscious repression of Indian psyche which is now giving rise to the widespread political violence and hysteria amongst us. And the price we are paying is immeasurable. Our conservative ideologues, intellectuals and politicians (who are the self-proclaimed guardians of Indian culture) should know that paradoxically it is they who are taking this country to catastrophe (their claim to the contrary), while they should—as true conservatives—conserve creatively what should be conserved, which means, destroying what is barbaric and demonic. All civilizations have barbarism: to encounter this, and remedy us from this, is the true politics of conservatism (and not to shy away from it).

What we actually need is truly conservative politics. But I have not met a single true conservative thinker. Perhaps Ambedkar was a little bit.

7. The banality of evil

The renewed "blood and soil" ideology in indigenous garb is really the most alarming and dangerous sign of our time. Today we don't need concentration camps any more; they are now everywhere in our very midst, plainly exhibiting itself in the clear light of day, and we are increasingly growing accustomed to this "banality of evil". What is more alarming?: The terrifying manifestation of evil in exceptional "sites", or, this quotidian manifestation of evil in all its banality, which we have learnt to accept as the necessarily constitutive element of the fabric of our daily existence? The most pitiable sight is that when an intellectual (the poet, the philosopher, the scholar, the University teacher or the student) mindlessly allows himself to be engulfed in this bottomless abyss, and become, instead of being the saviour of mankind, the very face of the evil.

In her much criticized but often misunderstood report on "The Banality of Evil", Hannah Arendt shows how the evil does not necessarily need to be incarnated in the figure of a terrifying face with its exceptional power and force, but that terrible evil can be manifested in the most stupid people, in the most banal way, in charlatans who pose as the spiritual saviours of the human race, though deep down they are just idiots, morons, imbeciles, impostors.

8. The wolf in sheep's guise

The world that we live now: charlatans are the teachers of the tender and the young in our holy institutions of learning; criminals are the judges in the courts; the wolves and foxes are our shepherds; crocodiles are our friends and well-wishers; imbeciles and morons are our spiritual path-openers; the stand-up comedians are our daily entertainers; thieves and robbers are our apostles; devils and their many headed serpents are our law-givers and law-executors; weeds are our daily bread; horrible cages of tortures and daily concentration camps are our royal castles; shameless and measureless mutual exploitation is the definition of our democracy; consensual rapes are the axioms of our love and immeasurably narcissistic exploitation of each other is the premise of our altruism; bloodless and tearless barbarism is the name of our civilisation.

9. Apocalypse

Beware of those wolves and foxes who pretend to be your shepherds but they are just waiting to attack you from behind, like thieves, in the dead of night.

As a good farmer knows how to distinguish the weeds from the crops and knows how to separate one from the other, so must we learn to separate thieves and robbers masquerading as apostles from the true apostles.

Beware of crocodiles, who weep in your distress, your tears are the capitals which they invest to fill their ever malicious stomachs.

As an experienced fisherman knows how to distinguish which fish dwells in what kind of water, so must we hunt down the false prophets and false guardians of culture from true prophets of our future.

10. Revolution on dove's feet

The true revolution comes neither with thunder and lightning nor with smoke and dust, but on "dove's feet". Murmuring at the edge of the world, rustling in the nocturnal hours of the day, humming in the remotest horizon of the sky, it silently and quietly transforms the world.

A true historian is one whose attentive gaze is concentrated on the murmurs, the rustlings, and the humming of revolutions: for what is decisive for human existence is not the nostalgia for our ancestors who have come to pass away, but looking back on the ruins of history, prepare a new world for our grandchildren to come.

11. My "politics"

Despite all my strong critiques of Marxist dogmatism (its unforgivable and tactful silence over the horrors of mass slaughter by Stalin and Mao, each one of them slaughtered many more than Hitler could, if one can alone evoke numbers here; the anti-intellectualism of the party and its autocratic behaviour; the refusal of the party to question the fundamental principles of its very discursive foundation; its neglect to deal with the questions of individual and life; its inadequate and dogmatic understanding of the question of religion etc), I have remained in the "left", more so at the level of practical and pragmatic politics, in the sense of what I consider to be the definition of "left": infinite contestation of any worldly hegemonies, and delegitimation of the rigidified established order of the world. This idea of the "left" consists of the task of remembering the unredeemed past of human history—not the glorious and triumphant past of mythic vitality, but the past of muffled cries and vanquished hopes—and, recognition of the exigency of an infinite future to be kept open for our grandchildren to be born, in the name of justice, beyond the closure of the solidified image of what already exists, in all its violence and unspeakable barbarism of useless suffering, as justified and legitimated. This is, in sum, what my "politics" is, if at all it can be termed as "politics".

For a deeper reason, I don't consider what people generally understand as "politics" (conditioned and practical negotiations between existing forces and powers of the world), as the ultimate horizon of human existence: my "politics" (mark the double quotation marks here!) is more ethically oriented, and therefore, I am not basically a political philosopher. For I think that there are dimensions and "experiences" of human existence that are not reducible to the conditioned negotiations of forces and powers: one encounters them only by renunciation of forces, and as such, they radically open us to that infinity which exceeds the inherent violence of force. Without this infinitude, politics itself loses its significance and importance for human existence, and everything would be totalized in the endless circular return of violence and the endless negotiation of forces. This is much more dangerous—and nothing can be more dangerous for historical humanity than this totalitarianism—than the politics of either right or left. A radical left politics must be attentive to this danger of totalitarianism from which—and history stands as witness to countless examples of this—itself has not been uncontaminated, and it itself has in fact left behind for the historical humanity ruins and graves of the oppressed. If the left has still to make sense for us—"we" the inheritors of the ruins and graves of history (rather than being inheritors of the glorious past)—then it must learn this terrible and terrible lesson from history, and must have a historical sense, a historical sense that it otherwise is so proud to have already possessed.

12. Ozymandias

Every worldly hegemonic order commonly shares and nurtures this one illusion: that its order is eternal and permanent. So each sovereign builds up colossal monuments in his name which will eternally praise the glory of his name. He thus competes with God, or at least sees himself as the divine representative on earth: as innumerable angels with their gossamer wings sing the hymns and praise the name of the Lord, so the sovereign on earth too has around him inspired and ecstatic poets and intellectuals who glorify these monuments which vanity builds up. To these sovereigns and ecstatic poets Ozymandias says:

> My name is Ozymandias, the King of Kings:
> Look on my works, ye mighty, and despair! (P.B. Shelley)

13. A psychological study of fascism

Every hegemonic order—which are often led by murderers of humanity—invariably have some charlatans and imbeciles (they call themselves "scholar", "intellectual" or "philosopher") who are always ready, for some petty profits, to sell their souls to these devils. They glorify and justify with all their intellectual weapons at their disposal these barbaric regimes that name themselves as "culture" or "civilisation". These " intellectuals" adore those fascists because at heart they themselves want to be like these murderers but they are too timid, too much like those wet cats; so they fantasise, and project their fantasies into those "strong" and " authoritarian" leaders (which means those who are capable of barbaric acts of violence and cruelty) and glorify them: there is, in this fantasy, lies the most terrible and most perverse form of repressed sexuality! So they magnify, through the magnifying glass of their fantastication, these authoritarian personalities: these so-called intellectuals of humanity call these "great" leaders "messiah", " the epochal man", "the millennium man" , or " the saviour of humanity"! And we know who they actually are, we who know how to read "documents of barbarism" (Walter Benjamin), we who alone inaugurate new history on the ruins of civilisation!

14. On Ambedkar's death anniversary

While a Dalit has been repressed in all possible domains—economy, politics, sports, arts etc.—no domain is more difficult for a Dalit to penetrate than into the domain of knowledge: Ambedkar, more than anyone, was extremely sensitive about this. In no other domain is Brahmanism more repressive than in the domain of knowledge, not because this repression is the most visible but precisely because it is the least visible of all: it is here Brahmanism operates in the most cunning manner possible; it is here Brahmanism is strongest and most jealous and most conservative; and it is here Brahmanism is the very best! This is why it was important for Ambedkar—and he pursued this in the most persistent, patient and rigorous manner possible—to decisively attack the order of knowledge: we must beat them; this is the most effective strategy possible, in precisely in that domain where our adversary is the best. In a game of chess, the attacks upon the pieces, major or minor, are unleashed only as necessary, ineluctable moments in order to checkmate the king, so in a case where you have checkmated the king without killing any piece at all, the game is over.

This is why it is absolutely important for a Dalit working in the intellectual domain to deconstruct the order of knowledge. Here there is a deadly double-bind, an aporia, a trap set up by the adversary in whom often a Dalit intellectual falls. This is the double bind:

1. In her eagerness to attack the order of knowledge/discourse, she very consciously constitutes herself as a 'Dalit intellectual', and often this leads to a ghettoization, which—not surprisingly—serves the interests of the hegemonic order: the hegemonic order happily allows the discourse called 'Dalit studies' while depriving it of all its militant, radical possibilities (something like that happens with Marxism: it is all fine to teach Marxism in the syllabus, teach in the class, now and then write a little book; but the moment she wants to transform the world, all hell is let loose!), and therefore, you will see all these Brahmins and intellectuals with Brahminical mindset happily teaching Dalit studies, guiding PhD theses, but they have actually remained politically obscurantist, extremely conservative otherwise (I know many such people who hate Dalits but their research students are Dalits, and their indignation is often furtively seen in what Freud calls ' the slip of the tongue'), and they reduce Dalit intellectuals only to be fit to do ' Dalit studies' (something like that happens with feminism: often you will see people get worried the moment a woman seeks to contribute something other than to the study of feminism, as if women can only be feminists and nothing else, as if feminism is not great and nothing much). Therefore it is necessary for a Dalit not to do just 'Dalit studies' (this I have learned from an extremely tender age in my precious manner) but enter everywhere, especially those places where Brahmanism rules sovereign. Unfortunately, even Dalit intellectuals who are dogmatically ' Dalits', consider that it is absolutely normative for any Dalit person to do only ' Dalit studies' , and if they find someone like me, they think I have betrayed the great cause, and that I have become the apologist of the hegemonic order. These dogmatic, militant, orthodox

Dalit intellectuals precisely thereby play into the very hands of the hegemonic order: Dalits must touch nothing apart from 'Dalit Studies'!

2. The opposite trap is this: there should not be anything called 'Dalit studies'. We should all, being equal, equally be part of one universal order. The cunning version of recent Hindutva thinking propagates this: there is a universality, only one—and thus homogeneous and equal—where everyone must belong to it, and which is a Hindu nation, in which case ' Hindu' is not a specific religion/cult/sect but, what they call (they think it is a smart move, but it is a downright cheap move)a ' way of life': ' Hindu' signifies a way of life, of being in the universal (some charlatans started calling it ' cosmopolitanism' or 'local cosmopolitanism': it is just a sleigh of the hand), in harmony and equality. We must all be included, under the law of the Hindu way of life which has certain visible symbols—an anthem, a certain slogan, certain bird and animal etc. But anyone who is little intelligent will see through this cheap trick: it is the whole trick of including-excluding. I call this trick 'inclusive exclusion'. In a great way, this whole trick is also the trick that has been exercised by patriarchy for thousands of years: it too has a concept of the universal—a concept 'man' which is made homogenous with humanity—but it is a downright lie, a false universality, which only impostors think that it is a smart move (chess is always a nice analogy even here!), but actually it is a crude, cheap, and imbecile move.

Therefore, it is good for a Dalit intellectual to be aware of these traps, of this double bind, and of the cunnings set up by the hegemonic order. It is necessary, in a strategic and yet in an unforeseeable manner, to contaminate the order of knowledge, and introduce, surreptitiously—with lot of cunning and intelligence and fortitude—the indigestible heterogeneities into the existing order of knowledge without reducing ourselves to a ghetto which the dominant order sets for us: neither succumb to the false universality, nor reduce ourselves to the ghetto—an impossible, but necessary task of all Dalit politics. Neither 'this' nor 'that' but think outside these oppositions. This is because by definition a Dalit—like the proletariat or like women—is a destabilizing element which touches the untouchable and un-touches the touchable, and in that process, thereby, destabilizing its own temptation to posit itself as substantial self-identity, as another hegemonic order in turn. Marx is therefore interesting: proletariat is not one class among other classes; it is a class that *de-classes* all classes and *de-classes* itself. Only then there will be a truly classless society. This is what Marx called, in his messianic manner, 'communist society'!

15. The apocalyptic cry

I just hope and pray that this intellectual space will survive for four more years. While the building and the name—and some other things instead of what have now—will remain, the spirit—which is the only decisive thing—may suffer complete shipwreck!

Everything is crumbling down: its beautiful conventions that once used to nourish the ethics of equality and democracy are now broken to pieces as 'flies to wanton boys' who they 'kill for sport'(Shakespeare, *King Lear*); the whole space of critical thinking and interrogation is now looking like a sand castle, and is now reduced to a mere servile instrument at the service of a destructive purpose; those who are supposed to be apostles and martyrs are now devil's advocates who sit in the front row and glorify the glory of the princes of the world.

It sounds criminal and barbaric—as the philosopher Adorno once said—to write poetry in these barbaric times! All our poetry has to now become an immense, apocalyptic cry against a pitiless, savage sky!

16. The cry

Every word that comes out of my mouth these days is a cry.

17. *U-topos*

In today's engineered world of mass consumption, poets and philosophers have less of a "place" than ever before. Its instrumental rationality can tolerate poetry only if it serves as our entertainment, that is: temporary relief from the anxiety of work-pressures, and instant gratifications of the senses so that the following day we are fit for work again.

Very few people notice this obvious thing that the concept of the holiday—which all of us celebrate as blessings that come at the end of every week—is the 'theological' or 'religious' conception par excellence: of all days of the week, the day of rest is holy, because God himself has rested on that day. This is why the seventh day is the most important day of the week, as the day of Sabbath being the most blessed day of the year. Our whole existence is sanctified on that day.

Today's secular world of mass consumption abuses this profound theological idea of the Sabbath, and reduces it to the mere temporary interval between two weeks of work, filling this interval not with holiness and blessedness, but with hedonistic cheap entertainments. Poetry and philosophy, in two different ways, are contemplation of the holy. And no doubt, in today's secular world of mass consumption, poetry—let alone philosophy—can only have its use only as entertainment.

18. Barbarism of poetry

We 'academics' and 'intellectuals' are often condemned as irresponsible, as mere arm-chaired university professors who do nothing to change the world, and we ourselves never cease feeling guilty and condemn ourselves too in similar terms. For long I have been defending myself for being one of those 'academics' and 'professors', and more than others I have the reason to defend myself, someone who researches on some hermetic and austere philosophical and theological questions which appear to have no consequence for the immediately existing world (why don't I contribute to the Assamese intellectual community? Why don't I do Dalit studies? Why don't I contribute to Indian philosophy? So objections multiply manifold!). When the world around me is going up in flames, I am reading a 5th century theological treatise: am I not irresponsible?

Interestingly, these days when the full brutal force of the state apparatus is falling into this little irresponsible place called 'University', especially on a little place of 1000 acres land wherein I am now writing this post, I feel for the first time that I don't need to defend myself, for everything is now obvious in its blinding and dazzling clarity. What is the most indigestible and the most disgusting space in today's stage of world-historical politics than this little place called 'university'? Negatively, this very disgust and repulsion with which the immense force of the overwhelming world-apparatus is forcing itself to destroy this inhospitable space called 'University': this shows, in more clarity than everything else, that this irresponsible behaviour of these irresponsibly thinking people called 'academics' are precisely those people who must be the most responsible people in today's world. The repulsion with which the world seeks to destroy the university life—the life of thinking and questioning—shows that, after all, our thinking is not inconsequential: the consequence is that the university life is the only inhospitable place in today's world! Inhospitability: this is the consequence (otherwise they would have spared Universities from their brutal force)! Thinking is inhospitable for today's world of planetary domination, and the paradox is that it is precisely this useless, inhospitable, inconsequential and irresponsible behaviour called 'thinking' that constitutes precisely the highest responsibility, and keeps the world of planetary domination open, in a fragile and tragic way though, to the last moment of the apocalyptic end of the world.

Nothing is more fragile than thinking, like love! And yet, it is this weakness and precariousness wherein lies the highest vocation of human existence! The most beautiful phenomena are fragile: whether flowers or children, love or thinking; the deepest depth of human existence, called 'the heart', is the most fragile thing, and yet, this fragility alone constitutes the meaning of existence. The paradox is that it is precisely this fragility which poses the greatest dangers and repulsion for the world-hegemonic forces. They want us, every one of us, to be thoughtless—that means—inhuman monsters who will serve to rule the immense machine of the world political-economic domination. Look at India these days: a few thousand young students and some academics in one or two universities of one of the biggest democracies in the world are fighting the tragic and lonely battle to its final consequence, and the whole nation is just looking at this spectacle, even without pity, but with threats of rapes and murder!

Therefore what Adorno says after Auschwitz is just the point I made: it is irresponsible and barbaric to write poetry after Auschwitz (it is irresponsible to devote one's life to a 5th century theological treatise when the world is burning!), and yet—lo!—how to think of Auschwitz today without Paul Celan?

19. Catastrophe and history

The 18th century and early 19th century philosophy of history is optimistically founded upon the principle of progress. From Leibniz's 'the best of all possible worlds' to Hegelian grand world-historical march of triumph, there was the faith that the world was increasingly becoming better, almost reaching or have already reached, the perfection of humanity. In the early 20th century that saw two world wars, massacre of six million Jews and much more in Stalin's Russia and in China, all that optimism has broken into thousand pieces. The theodicy of history of nineteenth century has to be given up, and was replaced with the catastrophic-apocalyptic vision of history. In the later part of the century the world then was only starting to recover, or at least thinking to start recovering from the devastation, these early decades of the new millennium are again seeing demonic forces of evil unleashed on the burning stage of history. Look at the last 16 years of this new millennium, everywhere the world is going up in flames: human suffering—and also the suffering of nature—knows now no bound and limit the measurelessness and extremity of which now defies any expression in human language. Nothing is permitting any hope that the world and the human race is becoming better and progressive, more 'civilized' and 'cultured', despite unprecedented and prodigious innovations in technology and scientific knowledge. As if an irresistible tempest, beyond the prodigious powers of the human race, is forcing the whole human world to an ineluctable catastrophe. There is no turning back: a blind and terrible force of necessity seems to be at work, invisible and impervious to the human reason, a necessity that has become necessity precisely out of the abuse of abyssal human freedom.

Will humanity come to the sober reflection of what it has done, to the world, to this tiny planet of the limitless universe, and to itself? Or perhaps, it is too late…

20. Fantastication

In the most proximate manner, human beings constantly live on inversions: what they consider to be 'truth' in the name of which every action, even the most barbaric ones, can be justified, is most often nothing but certain fabulization; and then they come to debase the truth as actuality to the dustbin of history. What makes fabulization and mythologisation possible is fantastication: fantastication fascinates human beings, and they get intoxicated in it, and in turn produce more and more fantastication. Once an idol has been raised on the stage of history—a political leader who is actually a tyrant and murderer of humanity, a pop-culture celebrity, etc.—an idolization where at best the fantastication is at work, from that time onwards everything the idol does, even if he attempts to annihilate a whole human race with the extremity of barbarism possible (which is limitless and measureless), everything the idol does appears beautiful, good and truth par excellence.

When one looks at this whole panorama of human history, one can't but become sick unto death with despair! Only from singular and individual beings can something like goodness come at all. These individual are precisely those 'remnants' that keep in reserve the human world from its complete annihilation in catastrophes.

21. The barbarism of the modern age

The barbarism of our contemporary civilization knows no measure and lacks any limit. We, living now, don't want to confront the pitiless cruelties of the modern civilization, and out of sheer arrogance of being able to pass judgment upon other epochs and other cultures (the privilege of being the latecomer), throw the immense piles of our condemnation upon what we call 'the medieval age'. Anyone who is not blinded by the prejudices of the age in which one lives, and has a good historical sensibility, will see that the middle age—in all its inquisitions and theological tyranny and crusades (there is no modern individual who can be like St Augustine!)—can measure up to the immeasurable technology of domination and savagery of the modern civilization with its measureless and useless suffering, and all these in the name of civility, culture and civilization. True, we no longer hang anyone with such cruelty, anyone whom we don't like, but we—without guilt—can destroy an unaccountable number of human beings (and other beings—animals and birds) using gas, with a smile on our lips and call ourselves 'democratic' and 'communist'. No medieval individual, even the cruellest inquisitor, could even dream of such a thing: this fantasy called 'democracy' which can kill six million Jews and 'communism' that killed numberless ones! It is good to have bit of historical sense, and to be able to pass judgment on the violence of history, and not to be prejudiced by the age in which we live!

22. Slave morality

The fundamental characteristic of the Brahminical order—more precisely the political order—is based on what Nietzsche calls "resentment" or "slave morality" whose fundamental category is negation: it can't think of affirmation in its purity. This is why

Buddha's *Ahimsa*—which is the purest form of affirmation—is the decisive break from the Brahminical order. The result is for everyone to see: Buddhism was persecuted and was driven away; it had to go to other shores to be nourished therein! Buddhism is the greatest contribution that India could ever have made to the human race (not yoga or software): now we cannot really say that Buddhism belongs to India! Immediately after its birth, within the very first few centuries, it was driven out fully packed (there was anyway no India, then).

The deeprooted *resentment* of the Brahminical order is the decisive source of the violence of the Brahminical Hinduism. The unspeakable horror of violence that has been perpetuated over millenniums makes one's hermeneutic of history into essentially a "hermeneutic of suspicion" (Paul Ricour). But this critical hermeneutic must already be opened in the purest gesture of affirmation so that we don't end up in the very vicious and violent circle of negations that have paralysed the Brahminical Hinduism!

23. Politics without ethics

What we need now, apart from the habitual modes of our contestation and protests, is thinking the political itself, which itself is the political gesture par excellence: we must introduce thinking into politics, and ideas into politics, not as mere guiding principle for practical political decision but to re-think anew the idea of the political itself as a new mode of contestation, that is, to do politics at a new level, at another level, and give it more than one language, new ones apart from what already exists.

This would demand interrogating the very concept of politics that exists today, and to think that which, while exceeding politics—we may call it ethical—makes politics possible and necessary. The terror and danger of politics as it exists lies in its inability to think; there is an idiocy in politics—by which I mean thoughtlessness—which makes politics a terrifying monster. The two world wars, destruction of six million Jews, a lot more under Stalin and Mao: these are only symptoms of thoughtlessness. Someone who worships a Hitler or Stalin, to name only the most prominent names, will go blind: they project their phantasm into those figures and once that happens, anything Hitler will say or do is not only acceptable but supremely good, *the* good, even if it demands annihilation of six million Jews!

Politics without ethics is the most terrifying monster humanity can ever conceive: all savageries and barbarism of human history are due to politics without ethics! To introduce the ethical—as the idea of infinity and infinite justice—in relation to the political and in excess to it: this is what a philosopher, an intellectual, an academic must do. This has the prerequisite that the philosopher and the scholar must strictly dissociate himself from the princes of the world, and ought never come even remotely closer to the worldly sovereign powers. The politics of the administration and the establishment, of the state and of the ruling ideology, can never be—by definition—the politics of the philosopher and of the academic. We too do politics, but it is a different politics: it is the infinite politics and infinite contestation in the name of an infinite idea! We can call it 'justice' or ' truth'.

24. Radical evil

What renders the demonic forces malicious and ravenous is their tacit knowledge that their rule is only transitory: hence is their hunger to attain being once and for all which constantly eludes them. More this eternal hunger shows their impotence, more is this hunger inflamed, like a forest fire that annihilates without expiation: this is, as Schelling shows, the radical evil. Only a fire of love that expiates without annihilation can be victorious over radical evil. Love is the liquid fire, the fire of water, that nourishes life and is before, as it is after, of the distinction between good and evil, and hence is the Good par excellence!

That is why confronting the forces of radical evil, we must at once maintain the ethical superiority over demonic powers of the earth, and vanquish them with the fire that gives warmth and fecundity to life. To expiate without bloodshed: this is the secret teaching of religion worthy of its name!

25. The unconditional justice

As a dying man wants life, so the oppressed ones clamour for justice! Our existence, in its very finitude, does not want to be exhausted in mere negotiations for conditioned-practical rights. Only infinity saturates and consummates our existence. This is why justice is the infinite idea par excellence!

26. Hope is the venturing beyond

To speak is to risk one's own existence, and yet, it is also the movement beyond by traversing the realm of death.

He who does not speak knows no hope, for hope is the venturing beyond into the unknown.

27. Blindness at noon

The fundamental impoverishment of the modern individual is not just his/her inability to give but his/her inability to receive, foremost its very being, its very life: hence is the restlessness and the closure of the modern 'man'. The totalitarian character of modern humanity, its aggressive assertion of itself in the midst of beings, is at once its utter depletion. The yawning abyss of this depletion, which makes the lust of modern humanity ever more insatiable, can never be fulfilled by inhabiting on this earth and on other planets as the sovereign being but would lead it, contra to its desire and mastery, to the catastrophic annihilation of all life. The developments in the world-historical politics today exhibit this logic in more naked brutality than ever before. But humanity, left to itself—which only makes it demonic—never learns its foolishness and blindness. With its very naked eyes, it can't see!

28. Tragic thought

While reading a fascinating book on the relation of church and state in early Christianity I am quite surprised by what it reveals to me: that in every historical epoch, there is the hegemonic political power, there are opportunists and pseudo-intellectuals who daily wash the feet of the prince, and there are those few courageous heroic individuals, persecuted and burnt alive, who defend the truth. This seems to be invariant logic through all vagaries of human history. And there is no end to this bloodshed till human history continues to catastrophe unless intervention takes place from a wholly other place. Man, on his own account, does not appear to have the power to halt this irresistible movement of history. Left alone to himself, man is the demon: he does not know at what time he has crossed the limit and brought the power of fate. Greek tragedy is all about this and nothing but this.

29. Conflagration

At one other historical moment, at least in last 50 years, Dalits are as oppressed, maltreated and slaughtered as now. Where can you raise the question of justice and equality?: All 'legitimate' authority has either become corrupt, or is incompetent to effectuate justice even in the domain of the law, that is, in the domain of conditioned effectuation. SC Commission, whose head is generally a political appointment, does not have any binding power; the court judges are now increasingly replaced by their men; constitutional rules are only applied where they serve the interests of hegemonic force; even soon to be the President of India—the most important individual of this nation—who will be a Dalit, is also their man! They can do anything, they are doing everything: slaughter, harass, and treat Dalits like the way people treat street animals, kicking on the butt as they treat donkeys ...the whole world is just looking on!

A movement has to erupt from Dalits: an immense movement, like the forest fire, like a wrathful conflagration, even if it takes two decades or three decades! When the barbarism on the stage of millennium long history is extreme, the claim of justice also has to be absolute and unconditional: then you don't count time in the clock; you stop the clock, bring it to its halt, and begin an absolutely new time.

30. The cry of justice

My intense political engagements for sometime have made me stronger, more vigorous, liberated and joyous. Though by temperament I am "private" and solitary who loves to do his intellectual work behind closed doors and invisibly at night—and this "public intellectual" does not suit me—at one instance I decided to speak up, and recognize my responsibility to speak for infinite justice.

This claim for justice demands speech, even though its speech has to tremble under the weight of violence (what a trembling speech it is!): such speech, an infinite speech that it must be, can no longer remain to be the patient speech of the victorious and triumphant (the administrative speech of the bureaucrats and engineers), but an infinite and impatient cry, even though it is only muffled, even though it sounds like mere murmur of the elements, like the voices of the sea and the wind on the desert! Even though the cry has not yet become music but only a shattered speech, still the "stones too [must] cry out", justice must still be given back its infinity: the resonance of the cry! This cry exceeds—like the ecstasy of mere existence that rustles at this hither side of the world, at the elemental depth of the earth—all grammatical (phonological-syntactic-morphological) logic of language. Justice is the ecstasy of language that makes the *morphé* of the world amorphous, and delivers the synchrony of syntactic speech to the stammering diachrony of the cry! Justice, by its very axiom, is diachronic: the event of diastases that interrupts the continuum of the hegemonic tradition that is ruled by the violence of the triumphant force, and apocalyptically burst it asunder. Justice demands revolution (that is, radical transformation, and not a continuous transition to an ever new point on the homogenous-evolutionary scale), which also means de-volution: impossibility of evolution, and impossibility of return of the wheel!

This is why the uses of the word "justice" and "truth" by those who put the whole stake of their life on the hegemonic regime (they also like to use these words) are absolutely unjust and false, mere abuses of these words: in its very presence as hegemonic force, the regime has to reproduce itself on a continuous transition to an ever new point on the homogeneous–evolutionary scale. That is why "the regime is always wrong" (Erik Peterson), and unjust, and false; it, by definition, can't know what justice truly is, and therefore, the regime is the true obscurantist par excellence: it obscures the absolute heterogeneity of justice, the blinding lucidity of the unconditional and the shrilling cry of the diachrony; it has to fabricate and make truth out of fable, and make justice out of injustice, because the regime in force always needs legitimacy. While the time of the unconditional justice is absolute heterogeneity of eternity over time (an instance that arrests the time), the "justice" of the established regime is, what Walter Benjamin calls, "homogeneous empty time" which only seeks, in the name of "justice", legitimacy of its hegemonic domination.

The so-called intellectuals—who are charlatans at best—who use these "philosophemes" to justify the hegemonic injustice, must be advised to clear up these ideas in their minds before they start using, or rather abusing them: that they are concerned with infinity, and each time infinity intervenes, it de-legitimates, shatters and suspends the totalizing order of the law; and as such, they have nothing to do with legitimation, but rather to do with delegitimation.

31. The birth to come

All nationalism is potentially totalitarian. To put into question the violence of the totalitarian order of nationalism does not mean being anti-nationalist; it means to keep the nation open to what exceeds all closures, to the very futurity of the nation. This is why etymologically the word nation means the birth to come!

32. Difference

Like Kierkegaard we must be able to distinguish between truth and truths: while the later are the conditioned realisation in the domain of quantitative distinction, the former is absolute heterogeneity and singularity, infinitely and qualitatively to be distinguished, the unconditional and non- negotiable demand par excellence.

We must intensify this difference rather than flatten them to a relative, conditioned difference: the latter always serves the interests of the hegemonic force.

Rustling, Murmuring, Humming

1. Moonlit night

Moonlit night:
A kiss on my lips –
- issh! This shameless wind!
You bring a
thousand memories of ancient days!

2. The hanging moon

Without a cry,
without a word,
without a tear,
or, even without a sigh
the yellow moon kept hanging
on the shadowy bough.

3. The hole

A hole
A big hole
An immense hole

A vast, measureless hole
This soul.

4. Exodus

I have become a stranger to the world,
a foreigner among my kin –
Nothing here, nothing, nothing, and nothing,
only a bleak, black, empty night
of soul –

5. Contemporeinty

To be old with the old,
to be a child with the playing child,
to be young with the blooming youth,
and yet, to be with none of them -
the wise one's secret!

6. The winter evening

Shivering to the core, the fruits drop dead-
Like the dead gods. The birds are frozen
in the lake. In my house, I have forgotten fire.
As if snows have turned all music into stones,
In the heavy air of last judgment, the vesper bell heard no more,
And the trees stand silent as from eternity, as the snows
Darken the world, the forest and the frozen lake.

What names I give myself, what names to the silence
That grows in the depth of my being, of what home and voice
To the void when gods have left—of what abyss:
This winter evening of extinguished light and fire!
Shivering to the core, I remain nameless from eternity,

Like the dead gods and the frozen fruits,
In my home all music has turned into petrified stone.

7. The round dance of stars

The round dance of stars –
Together we live, together we die!
In the lovely blue of your eyes I hear
The music of spheres,
And the resonance
Of the coming God.

Holy choir:
Angels of presence singing
Of the invisible other.
In the heart of the visible
Trembling, awaiting and longing,
Out of the mortal time, ecstatic—thus I remain!

The round dance of stars
Singing the glory of the one to come –
My invisible love!

8. Death

She is the fruit of my womb:
Nearer to me than I am to myself.

The dark-perfumed fruit of life,
An invisible dream –
Living in love without love, in life without life:
The song of stones, cries of the desert.
Solitude of the night's sky: starless, serene, deep!

She is the insomniac poet in my womb,
I am pregnant with her in a thousand suns;
Look: the world is rising in the east,

Like divine figures from stones and clay:
Flamed eyes, white arms, golden hair!

9. Origin

In her very open wound –
– That cut of flesh, that flesh of the caesura-
Between two melodious notes:
Undulating, She is crossing the invisible,
and exposing infinity unfixed:
to our inaccessible excess,
In the intimacy of distance!

10. Divine love

Snow on a summer morning
on my little hut,
and footsteps of my love nearing my door...
My hut is made of jewels of poverty
where silence speaks alone
and invisible shines over its dark sky.
I will dwell blissfully with my scarlet love
oblivious of the world
while the world whirls pass like lightning flash
on the desert of time.

11. Farewell

Meet me at the cross from where two roads depart from the other
for a word of one very last goodbye -
When the darkest hour of the night comes
and the world goes up in flames
come for just one more last time
for a kiss on my fevered lips.

12. Melancholy

Nothing, nothing here is in this desert
just one, vast, measureless nothing -
not it even a sigh, nor a tear, let alone a stammering word
just one vast melancholy wind faintly fainting away
in the distance, far and far away
where neither God nor man lives...

13. Judgment

What to say?: words stammer on my tongue...
Only if ashes could turn to flame the world,
and stones too cry out -
On the dazzling landscape of divine judgment…

Little Flower that I am

1. The language of the name

Writing is like Adamic naming. As the philosopher Walter Benjamin remarks: the beasts and fowls came up to Adam, bowed to receive their blessed names and blissfully jumped away in the landscape of paradise.

Through Adam the naming passes from God to creatures: to be able to name is not to be the owner's language, but to receive the very possibility of naming itself from God. It is God himself who names through Adam; it is He who moves the lips, and the blissful names erupt, like beautiful music, from Adam's mouth.

2. Joy ever ancient and ever new

Our deepest happiness—of what mystics and philosophers calls 'beatitude'—begins with the purity of our soul. We should not keep the purity of our soul in sight of, for the sake of, or in order to achieve happiness, but in such a way that this purity may become the very mode of our being that receives what comes to it gratuitously as a gift, namely, beatitude. This is similar to the way in which we ought to pray: not asking for something—'this' or 'that' thing (job, marriage, alleviation from suffering and sickness, etc.)—but praying to pray. This sounds difficult, unheard of a thing (what does this mean: this praying so as to be able to pray?: Yet, this is the only true prayer of the heart and soul), and yet, in another sense, it is also what is most simple, naked and radiant. This deep serenity so completely transfigures us that, if we persevere in the purity of the heart, it offers to us the highest that is possible for human existence. Attention, which love alone can give us (who is more attentive than the lover of the beloved?), must so permeate our inner mode of being that it becomes, one day, the very spontaneity of being, for being each time exceeds every act that we perform and the totality of all our acts and thoughts. People in the modern world are unhappy because they have forgotten how to receive and how to listen: only on the basis of this fundamental receptivity that happiness becomes for us a true possibility and actuality!

He who does not know how to and when to keep silence, knows not how and what to speak. The essential dimension of language is not the overabundance of words prattling away, but a deep, profound silence. An openness to silence in speech—in waiting—gives our language the essential; similarly, our receptivity in the purity of our heart gives our existence its essential happiness. The modern man is constantly hurrying up—nobody knows where and why—but just hurrying, not knowing how to wait. He misses thereby what is always already given to him, the joy "ever ancient and ever new" (St. Augustine), namely, our immemorial happiness, and the joy of having to exist at all.

3. The ecstasy of being

At times when at certain moments the soul attains a certain purity, there arrives an "ecstasy" which is at once so serene and light. We seem to be suddenly freed from the force of gravity, and there comes to permeate a feeling of equanimity for all sentient beings around us, a sense of blissfulness and blessedness in the atmospheric air that we breathe. We are suddenly freed from the weight of the past, and the burden of the uncertain future, and the darkness of the living present. Everything suddenly becomes transparent and is lit up, and we can see through the prism of our inner eye the deepest night of our soul clearing up and attaining lucidity that never came to it before.

Our profoundest happiness cannot be measured by the worldly things. We must rather measure the worldly things in light of the immeasurable. The law of the immeasurable is not the force of gravity but lucidity, simplicity and serenity that grants beforehand to things their gravity. As such, it infinitely exceeds any force or power of gravity. The definition of purity is the absence of gravity, a retreat or withdrawal from force. When this purity is attained, the soul comes to know the truth of its being: this truth is nothing other than a prism through which the ray of the eternal comes to pass.

4. *Lumen, melos, rhythmus*

It takes so long for the lucidity of existence to arrive to us (to most of us it never arrives), and that *melos* and the *rhythmus* to express it, in all its longing and yearning for the absolute beauty that, by the time it happens, one has already spent more than the substantial part of one's life. It becomes a matter of regret if we understand life purely quantitatively, that is, with the measures of the world; but, if we understand our life in sight of infinitude, even the fraction of a second that marks the very end of our life which is suffused with the effervescence of the *lumen*, makes it incalculably much more sense than if one is never to have any sense of it at all.

5. The song of phoenix

All that I need to do now—and in fact I have started doing this for sometime—is to bring all my ideas, thought, readings, materials and experiences to a certain point of concentration, of intensity and synthesis, to create something (a discourse, a body of works, works of creation—at once beautiful and rigorous) out of it, and with which to open up and illumine a world, "ever ancient and ever new"(Augustine), so that whatever I feel, think, read, write and experience (oh, how mortal is this being!) acquires the song of Phoenix—with all its measure, harmony and grace—so that it may reflect, as though through the pristine prism of crystal, the abyss of infinity in it, like the ethereal rays of the sun gleaming and glittering through the atmospheric air to give life its energy and sustenance.

6. Purity of the heart is to will one thing

'And the sea, like a wise man, is sufficient unto itself. Whether it lies like a child and amuses itself with its soft ripples as a child that plays with its mouth, or at noon lies like a drowsy thinker in carefree enjoyment and allows its gaze to wander over all, or in the night ponders deeply over its own being; whether in order to see what is going on, it cunningly conceals itself as though it no longer existed, or whether it rages in its own passion: the sea has a deep ground, it knows well enough what it knows. That which has that deep ground always knows this; but there is no sharing of this knowledge'. (Søren Kierkegaard)

7. Awaiting God

There occurs a stage in life when everything becomes slow and quiet: you speak slowly and softly and take more time to think of something with patience; the tumult and the clamour of the mad crowd reaches not your ear, and distract you not from the essential task. Rather than throwing yourself into the storm of history, or rushing headlong to God, you would rather wait with patience for God to come to you, even if it is a long time, for in eternity there is neither today nor tomorrow.

8. To be beautiful

Only a sincere, focused and attentive dedication—to " one thing needful" (Kierkegaard), a prayer-like work carried daily for a sustained period of time with patience, allowing time to the work to mature and to oneself to mature, detail and rigorous working out of the work with loving attention in detail, and above all, derive enjoyment and happiness as much as letting the existential transfiguration of oneself to take place: this alone can give rise to works of enduring value and this alone is worthy and significant.

We are so obsessed with transforming our CV (adding the number of pages) that we miss the decisive and the essential. We should rather be able to do the opposite: allowing transformation to occur for our existential self through fundamental works, and let our CV take care of itself, and believe me, you will not be disappointed.

Like the inner life of a profound human being, the work of significance too has its inner life. Our attention should be directed to that inner life of a work rather than its mere presence in the market of knowledge-production. The inner life of an essential work has something immortal about it, a quality so irreducible that the highest of human beings sacrifice their mere life. What we need is to strive towards immortality (not fame and name) that dedicates the transient life for an infinite task. It is this infinity that is the essence of beauty. To be beautiful is the vocation of our life. It is the privilege of art and philosophy that their sole concern is beauty itself—as an infinite task of creation. In these works of creation, divinity itself shimmers and radiates the world and makes the human world open to its redemption.

9. Wisdom is poverty

A teacher is most influential when he shows least anxiety to have adoring and revering disciples all around him, disciples who will form of school of thought in his name, disciples who will be his progeny...

The most difficult thing for a teacher is to learn that we must leave our students free from ourselves, learn to be abandoned by them, to dispossess them, and accept this poverty and dispossession as the highest blessing!

To be dispossessed: this is the definition of "wisdom"! While knowledge is possession, wisdom is poverty.

10. Discourse of indirection

When a philosopher does not write for others, he may create works that are of inexhaustible riches for others, but when he writes for others, either he is lying or he is in a state of deception and others profit nothing from him.

Therefore philosophical discourse is a discourse of indirection. Most of us don't have patience enough to undertake the long arduous voyage of the spirit; as in other matters as well, we want shortcuts even in matters of the spirit and intellect. But there are no shortcuts in philosophy, and this is not philosophy's fault. Philosophy does not shut itself away as a form of esoteric knowledge meant only for the few; rather, philosophy invites everyone and each one to examine his or her own life. As in all things in life that are of essential importance, this work too needs long preparation, spiritual disciplining, and being trained in the school of thought, of what the ancient Hellenistic philosophers used to call "askesis". There is no aristocracy or elitism here, unless one calls the poverty of *askesis* "aristocracy".

11. The absolute idea

I think I have arrived at the idea—that absolute idea, the idea of the absolute—for which I can live the rest of my life, the idea that constitutes my mission and vocation. The veil that obscured the light is now rent, and there is dawning a lucidity and clarity, along with it a divine joy, of knowledge of what is for me to do: I must now completely give myself to that absolute idea, and give it a new tongue that beautifully expresses it, for what is the task of a philosopher if not to attain an expression of the absolute?

12. The Good

It is necessary for a young person, especially someone who has something to do with matters intellectual or spiritual, to fix her gaze entirely on the one and one thing only, and steadily and firmly, without wavering and without looking for rewards from the external world, to go towards it, for such one thing can only have the meaning of infinity for her in relation to which everything else can only be relative, conditional, inessential.

Only the unconditional makes our mortal life not only just bearable but beautiful and worth living for; the rest , however glittering and seductive they may be, are only symptoms of despair; at one time or other they will abandon you to the "sickness unto despair"(Kierkegaard).

Only one thing is essential, which is the simplest thing in fact. The simplicity of the one thing is the definition of the Good—as Kierkegaard at one place says, which is also said in a different manner by Plato ("the Good beyond being") and Plotinus. That Good cannot be measured by goods in the world, by the values of economic equivalences, but precisely thereby—in still another sense—it is the highest value. That the highest value is also "valueless" for the external world: this paradox, or heterogeneity, is the truth of true life, and is its true meaning.

13. The irreducible heterogeneity

At the very moment when the world showers you with rewards for your achievements, you should be magnanimous enough to accept them with gratitude and humility, at the same time reminding yourself with the sternness of justice that they are only of temporal values, that the true reward is with the eternal, and is utter heterogeneity with the worldly rewards.

14. Only one thing is needful

I am dedicating the essential task of my God—the only one thing needful—to God, for everything that I am blessed with: happiness, love, thought and my existence itself—as gifts coming from Him alone. They are the rays from the fire of the Sun that gives warmth and vitality, but also scorches us and burns us if we become arrogant enough to cross the limit of our mortality.

In a deeper sense, the limitation of our mortality is no limitation at all, but rather is the very gift of life. It is only on the basis of our finitude can we be open to infinity. It is the measure of mortality that exposes us open to the bliss of the immeasurable.

Our mortality is not a cage of the law and of fate, but the very possibility of freedom and happiness. This freedom is the very ground of all that we mortals think, experience and do. It is true that this freedom can turn us into demons (which explains the possibility of radical evil: Schelling has something profound to say about this), but this is also the very condition of our being open to divinity and to our redemption.

Most of us don't know what to do with our lives and with ourselves. The task is to actualize this freedom in a measured way by regulating it to the establishment of justice and expression of love. When that happens, out life is fulfilled: we become like gods—happy, blessed, and blissful!

15. Reveries of a solitary walker

I always like to walk alone in the evening. On solitary walks what happens to me often—something that cannot happen if someone, even though the kindred soul, accompanies me—is what I call in my more philosophical writings as "event", event of an entirely peculiar sort. Questions that otherwise oppress and coerce me with the weight of their burdens, suddenly acquire wings of grace; the light of clarification, which otherwise I have to seek with the strenuous labor of thinking, suddenly comes to me in all its illumination and opening, questions like: what is the decisive and only one decisive vocation of my entire existence? I am already at the middle of my life, how much have I done to fulfil this decisive vocation? Am I on the right track? What about the status of my current work? What is the better, if there is any, way of proceeding? Is the comportment of myself to the world around me, to my immediate milieu (with all its messy-muddy-dingy politics), the right one? Am I too engulfed in it and so am I forgetting thereby to responsibly fulfil the vocation of my life?: Answers that I have to give to myself at the end of every day and at the end of my life—before myself and before God?

These are heavy questions, but on my solitary evening walks they come with all their gentleness and sweetness, like lovers come to their beloveds. In the light of the moon that illuminates without scorching us, under the shadows of tall trees when the world looks far away, questions come to me and answers are provided as "events". When I return home, I am all blessed: lucid, learning patience with existence, clarifying the opaqueness of life, realizing something existentially and spiritually higher than that is possible in the mundane immersion into life's multifarious and immediate problems.

One of my inspirations here is Rousseau. In his perhaps most beautiful, poetic and profound work *Reveries of a Solitary Walker*, Rousseau speaks of some of his most beautiful and most spiritual experiences, which are otherwise rare in his miserable and wretched life. These little things of life count the most (to take solitary night walks, to remain alone with oneself for a few hours of the day, to pray with utmost attention and loving concentration if one is religious, etc), precisely because we consider them as negligible, as only accessories of life (walking so as to lose weight, to remain fit: like everything else, everything is reduced to means to an end). As a result, life passes by unlived, and imperceptibly we grow old petty and cantankerous and die fruitlessly, because we see life upside down: what is highest we make it of lowest importance and what is lowest we elevate to the summit. Nobody can teach anyone "the art of living": it is to be acquired by living itself, living a life *as* life and not living life in the service of something else in life. In our modern world, what we don't know is living life, while we have everything else in life—wealth, worldly success, technological progress, planetary domination, and what not. But life we don't know, because we don't live life.

16. Dialectics at a stand still

From my childhood days my father indoctrinated me with this: that knowledge is the deepening of our inward soul and paradoxically, which is also the expansion of our intellectual-spiritual horizon. But when I have come to be an adult and, I found lot of knowledgeable scholars petty, sometimes even despicable and pitiable Lilliputians, I wondered: did my father teach me a wrong doctrine? After long years of deliberations, I realised that he was not wrong but that his doctrine needs few qualifiers.

See, there are two sorts of knowledge: one is what we generally call "knowledge": notional knowledge, or, better , instrumental knowledge ; but there is another knowledge, a higher knowledge, what I have to call it " existential knowledge", the essential knowledge, the holy knowledge whose origin is what Plato calls " erotic", the exposed or wounded knowledge—wounded by love—and exposed open, in humility, to what is excessive, which refuses any cognitive mastery or any appropriation/ possession. The former inflates us and thereby impoverishes us, and often makes us civilised barbarians; the later enriches us by dispropriating us and exposing us, out of finitude, to what indeed is infinite.

Often we don't know how to make the distinction between knowledge and knowledge, between false knowledge and true knowledge. Therefore being a teacher—whose job is to transmit/ translate—is a dangerous affair: not only is a teacher a dangerous man (who otherwise is so powerless and poor) but being a teacher oneself is the most dangerous of all. He can be demonic: he has an enormous power which is invisible and therefore he looks powerless and weak. But he is, in another and in a deep sense, the most powerful person whose appearance is all fragility and weakness.

It is imperative for a teacher to impart responsibly and pursue, infinitely, the infinite knowledge, which is paradoxical, because it is in pursuit of the impossible, namely, the non-knowledge. Therefore the greatest teacher of Greece makes the whole movement of dialectics (which is nothing but a method of *paideia*—a pedagogic method) come to a standstill at the precise moment of its fullness. When language comes to fulfilment, it is silence; but this silence, which is the mark of the highest human happiness on earth, is to be distinguished, by a responsible teacher, from the other silence, which is the negation of language.

17. Cosmopolitanism of spirits

In our desolate times when one is condemned to utter solitude and absence of communicability, the voices of those few friends from thousands of miles away, coming from a distance of seven seas and five continents, are my only solace. It is as if the territorial distance of geography does not lessen but rather nourishes the life of the spirit in a profound kinship and nearness beyond anything biological, racial, national, religious and linguistic. It is this cosmopolitanism of the spirit that seems to be the only hope in these hopeless nights.

18. Beauty and melancholy

My favourite flower is 'night jasmine': it blooms only at night—invisible from the light of the day—only to wither away in the morning. From my very early childhood days, and I don't remember since when (it looks so immemorial and ancient, as if I have lived since the beginning of the world, and will live till the extremity of the end of the world, and yet, this immense span of time is just flying away like a lightning flash, as if eternity is just an instance when time stands still and yet flies away at the same time too fast and too quick! A paradox!), I have remained the lover of just this one flower! A simple, little, wild flower that blooms by the roadside, its delicate petals are of purest white and its intoxicating perfume is perceptible only to her lover who loves her nocturnal existence; and when this lover wakes up in the morning, and sees the carpet of them below his feet on the wet grass of the autumn, their perfume enveloping his inner existence, he sees their incomparable beauty, attuned to that faint melancholy, that is the mode of all that is transient and evanescent, as if only the melancholy is beautiful, as if "the beauty of a landscape resides only in its melancholy"(Ahmet Rasim).

When I shifted to my current house, the first thing I noticed was the night jasmine tree at the entrance of the house. Every morning these days I wake up to inhale the intoxicating perfume of her existence, and somehow this melancholic feeling inevitably comes to me: my own existence is like this night jasmine, and that there is between us an immemorial intimacy beyond words, a love and a beauty whose profundity no words will ever express; and my love and my own inner existence is to remain secret and invisible, like the nocturnal existence of my beloved, from the light of manifestation. How can we say this?: There is nothing else in the world other than this absolutely simple, tiny, wild and nocturnal flower which is the emblem of my existence. She is what I am: a night jasmine! My beloved and I are one!

19. The Archimedean point

The only thing I can do to maintain my sanity these insane days is to find, in the middle of all the "storm and stress", an enduring point that gives certain calm fixity to my inner existence. I see before me the last embers of a world dying in the evening sky, and the last leaves of dying trees falling on the barren earth, and are tossed to and fro by an irresistible tempest falling from a pitiless sky; and I see the redemptive hopes of the renewal of the world float like tiny rudderless boats in the turbulence of a measureless ocean. What an individual, with the last remnant of the spiritual in him, can do against the triumphal march of the civilized barbarism that irresistibly animates the entire movement of world-becoming? "I have nothing better to do than, where possible, augment what is my own and has been left to me, to distil and redistill my own individuality" (Goethe). The only thing for me to do is to discover and rediscover and to remain attached to that axis around which my life is to move—the only condition of remaining true to oneself in the midst of this blazing landscape, and amidst this great conflagration.

20. Tragic knowledge

When we look back memories of the past flash like lightning before our eyes and we suddenly recognise the past long forgotten, even our pain and wounds appear in the light of redemption. We look at them with a serene melancholic gaze, and accept them as an ineluctable part of our own existence: those incomparable faces we loved once; those wounds that once consumed our heart; those ordinary events of joy that have disappeared forever on the sands of time, only to remain traces on the yellow pages of dusty albums; and those people who once shared their youth with us, and now have that left long behind—all that, long lost, looks in our remembrance like pale lights gleaming from another world, distant and remote, now more beautiful than ever, a beauty tinged with such a sadness that it is closer to the muteness of animals than to the words of an eloquent speaker. In this serene contemplation of our past, the whole past landscape appears like the whole of life gathering to a single moment in the eyes of the dying man: we forgive the unforgivable; we ask forgiveness for the irremissible pain we once caused others; we thank those who loved us, even if just for a single day, and most of whom we will never again encounter again in this voyage of life, they who now enrich the lives of others.

Like the solitary man who is just returning from the bank of that great river, watching the last embers of the setting sun glistening on the waves blood red, and is returning home with that unspeakable and unnameable sadness of joy, we too return—after our melancholic joy of memory—to our quotidian life, renewed and deepened in the inwardness of our heart, with a new light and new knowledge. A tragic knowledge!

21. The mustard seed

I cannot escape marking this remarkable change taking place within me: this deepening of the inward gaze and withdrawal from the external world; this simplification and almost ascetic-like life which I lead; this constant desire to be invisible from the public/social relations, and to retreat to a small place, quiet and silent, for some contemplation and peace; this minimization of a social circle of friends, which is now reducing almost to nothing, apart from just one or two friends (I don't seem to have much of this need!).

As opposed to this *apatheia* with respect to the external world, what is happening, on the other hand, is an intensification of a new desire, overflowing and outpouring, for that which is nearer to me than myself, and more distant than all distances, a desire for the infinite and essential; a desire for something deeper than all the depth the world has, and for a light of knowledge that so gleams and glints that it becomes dark like the night: the husk falls so that the seed, naked and abandoned, can sprout, bursting out its shell; and the mustard seed grows towards the lovely blue of the sky, while the earth groans and writhes in agony.

22. Night thought: the beautiful!

The most beautiful writing—of a poet, a mystic, or a philosopher—comes from beautiful thinking (or, beautiful experience!): someone who thinks beautifully, someone whose thinking constantly turns towards beauty, someone who experiences beauty, cannot but write beautifully! For at the secret origin of beautiful writing lies beauty itself: beauty calls up, from its invisible and inexhaustible wellspring, thinking to sing beauty. Can a thinking, whose origin itself is beauty, be other than beautiful itself? Only beautiful thinking makes its expression truly beautiful! An individual may know all about the techniques of artistic expression, still he remains only a craftsman. For someone who herself is called up by the vision of beauty, all these techniques are only preliminary necessity; they don't really constitute the essential of art: for the essential, she must have the genius—her eyes, her ears, her nose, her skin, her tongue and above all this beautiful place of the human being called 'heart': all attentive to beauty, and nothing but beauty—for beauty. For beauty is what makes, and what gives the human being it's highest happiness: it is beauty, above all, that makes us truly happy—in the highest and in the most noble sense. This highest happiness is what we name as "beatitude", the neighbour, or, the proximate word of "beauty". This is why, someone who has the vision of beauty must be happy, essentially and truly! This is a different happiness than what people generally associate "happiness" with: it is happiness in having seen beauty itself! In a very different sense—and I cannot really write about this without difficulty, one has to really undergo the voyage of experience himself or for herself—only beatific people, in the highest and noble sense, see the truly beautiful!

23. Ignorant knowing

When the Sophists floated like windbags, Socrates with his radical dialectical strategy made their arrogance and sophistry burst and made them go up like smoke. The sophistry of these Sophists could not withstand the radical ignorance of Socrates. That's how the declaration of the oracle got fulfilled: Socrates is the wisest of all because he of all is the most 'ignorant'! There is a wisdom or knowledge, the best that is possible, which consists of being 'ignorant': the whole dialectical movement, in all its paradox (knowing without knowledge), has its 'telos' this instance when knowledge comes to a 'standstill' and opens to something extraordinary in astonishment or marvel.

24. Humility

The first virtue that an individual who is seriously engaged with matters intellectual and spiritual (a writer, a scholar, a philosopher, a mystic) is humility and modesty, along which comes a certain cultivation of being ' incognito'; one must learn to carefully conceal one's knowledge and wisdom. Such an individual is like a child: simple, lucid and pure, like a crystal clear spring of water reflecting in its mirror the rays of eternity.

Here is a teaching from my half-literate mother: the tree which is fruitless, haughtily erects its head, while the fruitful tree, with so many fruits every year, keeps its head low, as if it is constantly waiting to receive blessings from heaven.

25. Infinite love

The true light of comprehension is in itself not knowledge in the strict sense, but a loving-knowledge or knowing-love. As such, it can only be paradoxical: it is at once a kind of non-knowing! It is all light, all love and all warmth: only in so far as it is infinite, it is a dark night—of the visible.

There is a beauty that becomes visible only when we learn to close our eyes: as we withdraw from the light of the world, the other light appears brighter ever to the point of abyss! He who has seen this abyss of light, sees nothing more and nothing else: the whole of existence becomes now a vast, measureless, ecstatic melody of lights.

26. The movement of infinity

The reason why our contemporary scholarship is so terribly boring and they lack all life and spirit is this: that he needs books to write a book, that his books originate solely from other books. As such, he is a scholar or a philosopher only when he sits down on his reading and writing chair-table; the rest of the time, he is everything else (a share market speculator, a politician in sight of power, a careerist in sight of the next promotion, etc) but not a philosopher. So when he takes an evening walk, he does not ever talk to the birds, trees and the sky, nor do they talk to him—the beauty of the moon escapes his gaze; everything, everything where certain truth may be manifested to him, evades him; his sole concern to just to remain fit and lose weight. If he reads books—and these days every literate person is a prodigious reader, especially in academics—it is either to write a book in his own name, or to entertain himself, to be relaxed, to take a break; as a result, nothing existentially transforms him: he remains the same person after reading the book as before: a careerist, a man of worldly profit, a seeker of entertainment, a bourgeois philistine.

When I read St. Augustine, or Kierkegaard or Simone Weil, what interests me is this: they never wrote a single sentence for the sake of mere publication; to be a scholar or a philosopher least interests them. There is another, something overwhelming and great, existential demand that they experience, and they need, or they are compelled, to express this truth in works; so the works are products of a profound need—to make manifest a truth that they have experienced. It does not matter whether one has written only one book, or, left behind a few precious aphorisms: what matters is making manifest of a truth that is existentially demanding and transforming.

I wonder these days: why I cannot be like this (not to be great like Kierkegaard: you must not misunderstand me)? I must allow, and work towards, an inward deepening and my existential transformation, and let rays of truth pass through me as through a prism, and then, if that truth claims to be expressed in works, let it be expressed in my works, in my life as much as in my books! I think this makes far more sense—even if I write just one book—than writing fifty books with no consequences, fifty books of a sterile mind in pursuit of worldly benefits. It is this thought that had been overwhelming me for the last few months, making me hesitate to write a single line, even though my spirit brims with ideas and thoughts. I have become miser of words. And on the other hand, I am undergoing unspeakable agony all these days for not writing—for writing is life—and yet, I refuse to write: I want the rays to envelop me, making me a mere instrument of communication, the rays of a fundamental idea that must bear all the consequences of life and death for me. I am in pursuit of an impossible that can occur only by a gratuitous gift or by an overwhelming grace: maybe it will never happen to me. But I must take the risk, and make another movement of life, the movement of infinity.

27. Humanity of the human

The profundity of human existence lies not so much in realising, or, accomplishing effectively, the possibilities that belong to humanity, but in keeping humanity open to, and welcoming—in hospitality and generosity, in gratitude and humility—what otherwise than mere human are: in other words, not only the other human being, but also divinity and other created beings. The truth of humanity is this originary openness of human existence. The responsibility of humanity is, therefore, not exhausted in realising the potentiality of humanity qua human-ness; we cannot understand this truth and responsibility without undergoing the certain peril of suffering where the very humanity comes to be at stake; the human must be called into question, even to be judged, or to be called to responsibility that cannot be wholly understood by any fixed, pre-given categories of human's self-understanding. This radical alterity where the violence of human's self-assertions and claim for sovereignty is to be put into question: how do we name it? I hesitate to name it as "reason" which itself is supposed to be a human potentiality, nor the power of action which leaves a hundred things undone to do one thing: then, what do we name it?

28. To philosophise therefore I am

However would I love to be a painter or a musician, and however I envy their ecstasy (they seem to me to live in " another world", and how much would I love to be there myself!), I have realised that I am basically meant to study philosophy, and hopefully to be a " philosopher" one day, and that it is this which my "destiny" is: with my contemplative temperament that submits every experience and every event to a certain manner of thinking , with my aptitude for sustained and patient examination of phenomena and with my vigilant insistence on sober prose. My inner being is not primarily one of ecstatic disposition, though I know enough ecstasy myself; I am primarily a contemplative that gives phenomena the expression of sober prose and of ideas: this is typical of what a philosopher does, as distinguished from an artist. Though I am much of a poet—about how I experience the world and how I write—the catalysis that transforms my experiences is primarily that of the contemplative, that means, "philosophical" one: it incessantly translates events into the language of ideas and ideality that transcends, by way of mortification, the temporal and spatial location of the events themselves. The whole inner concentration of my existence lies here: in this work of translation of events into the language of ideas.

29. Aristocracy in destitution

Someone who is engaged in some fundamental activity, that is, in a task that is infinite, must disregard or suspend to a great degree any concern with its immediate reception by others or its consequences for the immediate world. A painter who is making a painting, or, a philosopher who is engaged in philosophising, must disregard whether his viewer or his reader will understand him or not. This is why I am most often difficult: not because I enjoy the sophistry of being difficult, but because I need to invent an idiomatic expression whose sole desire, at least at the instance of writing, is to seize that absolutely singular thought that has to come at that absolutely singular moment; its sole desire is to maintain an absolute fidelity to an expression of truth in a language adequate to that event. I really don't have time to think about my reader, then; all my attention is concentrated on the event of thought and the language in which that event will come to pass, like a sword wounding the heart of language. The fidelity to this event, for me, is at any time more important than the question whether anyone understands me or not, for what will be necessary for my reader—to understand me—is at least to have the glimpse of that event for herself. It is this deeper understanding, which is deeper than what people generally call "understanding", is what I appreciate from my reader. It is always better for me that a few people understand me than everyone: this aristocracy of mine is of a different nature than what people call " elitism"; I am not elitist, writing for privileged few who know " theory"—frankly, contrary to my appearance, I hardly know many theories; I am rather an aristocratic of thought, of vision, of existential transformation—someone who assumes the risk of the vertigo which thought opens, at its limit, to the unthinkable and to the immeasurable. This is not elitism that has to do with privileges; it is the paradoxical aristocracy of poverty and destitution: it is aristocratic in its destitution; it is destitution in its aristocracy.

30. Only one thing that is necessary

It is absolutely and unconditionally important that an individual gives himself an unconditional and absolute task to his life, a task that cannot be exchanged with any other works of life, and is, hence, absolutely nonnegotiable and non-relative vocation: only one thing that is necessary! Otherwise a human life, consisting only of multitude—however big is the number—of relative works is only despair: after all, how long will you keep on living a life just by accumulating wealth, becoming successful and famous, feeding yourself on the love and friendship with other wretched human beings who are just like you, equally insecure and petty?: After all, wealth comes and goes, nothing is more insecure and precarious than fame and name, and human beings too come and go to and from your life like waves of the sea. Being hooked to anyone of the relative things of life, which are only quantitatively different, and thus bestowing on it the ultimate significance, as if it is the only thing that matters: nothing is more foolish than this! Only an absolute, nonnegotiable and unconditional vocation, one that will never enter into exchanges with any other worldly values, can redeem us from the fundamental despair that yawns, like an abyss, at the very centre of human existence. To grow mature—to respond to a questioning and thoughtful reader of mine—means to recognise this absolute necessity of life, and to be able to find, in absolute abandonment—when the individual faces that abyss all alone—that 'Archimedean point' (as Kierkegaard calls it) from which to view life, one's existence, and to give it a beatific and redeeming appearance.

31. The light of the world

One must bear knowledge as one bears one's smile: not to be weighted down by the nocturnal depth of knowledge, but to lighten up the world. As a smile transforms the gravity of existence into grace, so must our knowledge transfigure the weight of existence into light.

32. The fragile love

Everything begins in love. According to a certain Greek myth the most primordial God is Eros. In a certain Kabbalistic conception, God created the world not out of his power but out of love: out of his love, he renounced his overwhelming power, and let the world (which, in a way, is 'beside' him or 'outside' him) come into being. Love and power, then, are in-commensurable: there is no love without the least renunciation of power and violence. God made himself fragile, in a way, so that humanity and all that is created may come into being. Creation, then, does not bear so much the power of God than his fragility, his weakness, and abandonment.

In that sense, philosophy, which means love (love of wisdom), has less to do with knowledge than with love. Plato in his beautiful dialogue called *Symposium* makes Socrates put this into the mouth of a wise woman called Diotima: that philosopher is the most erotic individual, and philosophy itself is the highest form of eroticism. Knowledge gives power: there exists something like 'cognitive violence' that is the metaphysical ground of all violence that humanity is capable of. On the other hand, love demands renunciation of violence and power: love is non-knowledge. Socrates calls this non-knowledge 'ignorance'. Socrates is radically ignorant because he is, as philosopher, basically a lover! The philosopher is not a wise individual, not even a knowledgeable person: s/he is essentially an erotic being.

All our love—love of art, love of truth, love of other human beings and anything that exists—all these profane loves are reflections of that one primordial love. So when we love another human being, and find her beautiful, we see in her face reflections of the divine love and divine beauty. This is why we can be so irresistibly drawn and attracted to the beauty of another human being: that other human being, in all his singularity, even though for the rest of the world he may appear to be just ugly. They have not seen that beauty in him what "I" have seen in him: dim illumination of that divine spark that has created, and that ceaselessly creates the world for all eternity! Every time we love another human being, or any being, the world is as new as the first day of creation: every day of love is always the first day. Therefore love is the most ancient thing in the world, the oldest of all, and it is also, paradoxically, the youngest and newest of all: "Most ancient and ever new", as St. Augustine says.

In today's world of unspeakable violence—in the name of nation, for money and success, and violence of politics and religion—love alone, being so fragile, can transform the world, and renew creation. The human being, who according to the Bible is God's best creation, has the unique responsibility to all creatures of the world, not just for the creatures of his kind. Because he inherited from God the fragility of love: as God has to renounce his sovereignty, so the human being must renounce his sovereignty and autochthony, in the name of love, for the sake of creation and preservation of the world. The human being is given the gift of language—which otherwise only God can speak "let there be light"—so that each time the creation may arrive anew in language, which is always born out of love. This is because love is also the origin of human speech. In human speech the world awaits for redemption!

33. Nameless sadness

Sometimes one can't help feeling an unspeakable and unnameable sadness in all that exists, in all that is sentient and transient: a sadness that weeps in the perfume of flowers when I pass them; the profound sadness that slumbers, behind the daylight, at the heart of things, and when I wake up, after a nightmare and sit alone in the dark, that ever-existing sadness wakes up too yawning, and comes out from the dark depth of existence like vapour, as immaterial as undeniable is its existence; there is a wordless sadness in the humming of the remote sea as much as in singing of crickets in the silent nights of the countryside; there is this irreducible sadness in the monotonous, ever rambling sound of the clock at midnight as much as in the mute melancholy of a hungry cat that looks at my eyes with an incredible appeal that I can't not respond to; there is a hidden sigh in the angelic laughter of children too as much as in the beautiful smile of a beautiful woman, or in the rich wisdom of the old. As if everything that is created—the whole order of creation—is marked by that profound mournfulness: in the depth of the night as much as in the summit of the mountains, in the momentary glance of lightning as much in the always returning face of the moon in the evening! And all rise up to sing, in chorus, the mourning song within my little heart, weeping without consolation and without salvation, longing for that which it can't name!

Only the unconditional can redeem us from this measureless grief! Who knows there may be sadness, even if like a remnant, still resonating even in the heart of God?: He must have always been weeping too—for us, for me! The only thing we mortals can do—without trying to evade it in instant gratification of momentary pleasures (which today's world of mass consumption supplies inexhaustively), without running away from it and finding salvation in the cheap entertainments of modern man's creation—is to listen to the vast melody of melancholy in all that exists (without making it " pathological"), and to salvage from the order of creation those remaining of sparks, or lightning of infinite and eternal that still shine, dimly though and in a momentary manner, in the face of things, and in the human visage, and in the face of nature, and to let it come to expression, in human creations, to certain perfection and beauty and truth, and thereby reflect, in adoration and humility, the unconditional in all that is conditioned.

34. The flower that I am

Every day I look at two 'things' without a miss: flowers and the sky. I look at the flowers by the roadside, in my garden and in the gardens of my neighbours: as if they are born just to bloom, to beatify the world, and then—when that purpose is fulfilled—to wither away without an instance of delay. How beautiful is it to be a flower! When I was a little boy, I just wanted to be (like) a flower: so when the adults asked me 'what is the aim of my life', I used to answer: 'To be a flower!' (What a strange answer was it!).

Time passed. I grew up to be an adult: I wanted to be 'something' or 'someone'—a writer, a philosopher, or something like that! And something like that I have become. And now, looking back at the whole landscape of my life, my old dream has come back again: ' Just to be a flower—to bloom, to beatify, to perfume the world, and to wither away'; or, better, 'to remain the flower that I am, the flower that I have always been—and still I am '! Not the rose of the garden, or the orchid of the rich man, but that wild, nameless, white flower in the wilderness...

35. From the other shore

Sometimes I wonder why children and old people adore me! I have always been so hugely popular among them, especially with children!

As in every sphere of my life, here too I am the odd one: I am not a contemporary among my contemporaries; I am too young or too old; arriving too early or too late. I am the father of my father, and son of my son. I have the head of an old man, and heart of a child: like that of a child, my heart too flutters in the wind, wants to leap high just enough to touch heaven, and laughs like blessed angels. I know profound joy, as paradisiacal like that of children, but I also know the most intense abyss of melancholy that comes with knowledge.

Everywhere I am the odd man: that is why I am everywhere, fluttering in the blue depth of the sky with my invisible wings.

36. I have to let things go

At one moment I have to let things go: some painful memories of the past, my guilt that I could not be with my father during his last years, petty everyday politics of petty powers, every day nagging and cribbing that make my everyday strenuous and constraint my very freedom to be, weights of such other mundane torments etc.! I realized that let alone everyone, not even a single person I can make happy: I try to make someone happy, it leaves another unhappy; someone smiles, another cribs! I am really unfit for every day petty politics, I don't have that energy and diplomacy; and somehow I can't be too much involved in everyday practical affairs of a thousand minute things, I don't have much interest in it, and after a little bit of engagement my mind wanders to something else—to my work, for example! The quotidian life feels oppressive and constraining to me: I don't like to meet too many people, and all the time; I don't like to be visible all the time and to everyone. The truth is: the deepest core of my inner being is somehow not with, and not in the world; a purely 'human' world, consisting only of human artefacts and human relations constricts and suffocates me. In other words, I am not a 'human, too human' an individual: I need something outside the given world—I need flowers and the sky, and I need God!

So I have decided to let things go, or let things be, and thereby renouncing the desire to control too much the order of things.

I cannot change the world, and I can't change anyone, at least directly, but I can change myself little by little, and free myself from the bondage of the earth and cages of the world for my beloved God and to fulfil the God-given vocation of my life! For I have a mission, a vocation of life that I have to fulfil before I die! So I can't hope too much to linger on weights of everyday life. How long can I keep on fighting with people—most of them are just worthless and petty? How long I will keep running with others in the ladder of worldly success? How long can I keep breaking my head against everyday practical difficulties? They just seem unending. You get one success, another evokes your longing; you have just sorted out one difficulty of everyday life, and another just has begun; you have just dealt with one person, another difficult person is clamouring: oh, this is just unending, and if I involve myself too much into these numberless chaos, I will just lose my sanity, let alone fulfilling the vocation of my life.

I have to free myself for God! And I have to free myself for the essential work of life. And for that objective I have to set aside even my anxiety before death. When I look carefully at the history of my inner intellectual life, it appears to be nothing other than a long series of contemplation on death. Now it appears, death—this physical death of this earthly body—is really not of fundamental consequence—for anything and for anyone: the world will remain what it is to remain, with or without me; people will remain, after a few days of mourning, what they are to, with or without me. When one fulfils one and that great single vocation of life, in great love and in the name of God, then death will not sting me anymore. It does not really matter how long one lives: if I can fulfil the vocation of life tomorrow, I have no reason to live a single day more on this earth! If I don't do anything in one hundred years, what is life but despair? A long life is senseless: I prefer a short, beautiful life, with the work to do, and in adoration to God.

37. Tonight I will write the most beautiful words of my life

I have been sad for the last one year to see this beautiful institution collapse amidst many other valuable things in our national life; it has been painful to bear witness to the rise of dictatorship, the undeclared state of emergency in our national life, the robbing of basic rights of being 'human' and 'citizen', and the reduction of existence to mere lives, etc. I, then, wonder what I am supposed to do, as a responsible scholar and responsible citizen, knowing full well that all these will ultimately amount to nothing: how powerless is thinking—which is what I do—in facing the brute, barbaric powers of 'legitimate' authority, those powers that seize our throats with the force of violence, and annihilate our voice with their savagery.

I look at more or less similar situations in Nazi Germany, and looking for a clue, ask myself, what the intellectuals have done in those terrible, dark days when humanity was suffocated in the gas chambers? What Adorno, Benjamin, Bloch, Bonheoffer, Barth and so many others were doing? I read Bloch writing his massive masterpiece of many thousand pages on hope—one of the greatest books of the last century—while living an exiled life in America, working as a manual labourer, and his wife working as a domestic servant in others' houses, washing utensils and cleaning floors! And he wrote of hope! What madness! Bonheoffer undertook the most maddening and impossible plot to assassinate Hitler, and in turn being assassinated at the age of 39 (my age!) while writing his greatest book on ethics in jail waiting to be executed, and his last lines were, while he was being dragged to execution: 'This is just the beginning of my life'! And I read of Benjamin's extremely painful life—without a job, no money, a messy private life—leading to a desperate suicide while fleeing from the Nazis! And he was writing in those terrible days his greatest, and unfinished magnum opus on arcades of 19th century Paris! And I read how Barth, courageously, defended humanity before God against the barbarism of Hitler, and writing the many thousand pages long theological book on dogmatics which is considered only as second to Thomas Aquinas' *Summa.*

What am I doing? Should I give up thinking-writing-reading—this very life which is the only one I know—in this ruin of civilization when piles of rabbles are growing bigger and bigger in front of me? No, I will start writing tonight the very best book of my life, while the world is collapsing around me like the house of cards, and I will write, not of despair, but of hope against hope and hope contra all hopelessness, and I will write of abandonment, and of the joy of being and having, still going on affirming this humanity that I share with so many others…

Tonight I will start writing the best book of my life, the most beautiful sentence of my life! Lo!—I have already written it!

38. Who am I?: a little flower!

For a long time I have been wondering: what should I call myself? Or, how should I understand myself? A plethora of terms come to my mind: a teacher, an academic, a scholar, a writer, a thinker, a philosopher. What am I? So I take up one after another and examine each one in turn:

A teacher I am: it is the least ambiguous among all the terms, but what I basically do is covered only in a limited way by the term 'teacher'. I teach on the basis of what I do—reading-writing-thinking—and not vice-versa. Then comes the word 'academic': it is a term so technical, and so connected with the institution called 'University' that only with a great deal of constriction can I accommodate myself to it; I would rather like a more poetic term, free from any institutional designation, for what really puts my whole life at stake is less of an institution but rather that of destitution. Then comes the term 'scholar'. Who is the scholar?: Someone who knows a good/great deal, someone who primarily seeks knowledge; in other words, knowledge is his business. Is it my business/job too?: yes, but only to a certain extent, and that too not primarily. At a very fundamental level, I am basically not at all interested in knowledge and in knowing, but something else... 'A writer': yes, I do write; writing is my passion (oh, what does not happen—this agony and ecstasy—in writing!)! But it is a word nowadays and more or less is associated or confused with novelists, and with such writers (even journalists and poets), and I am not really that. 'A thinker': oh, how much I would like to associate myself with this term! But who does not think? Can there be a 'thinker'—as such? Then comes the term, the last in the list: 'the philosopher', which also happens to be my most favourite word. Yes, this strange thing called 'philosophy' is what is given to me (what a gift it is, from a source so invisible and generous!, as if philosophy has been decided for me from my birth, in a kind of immemorial manner), as the task and a vocation of my entire life. But will it not be too much—a pretension, or a vanity—to keep the word 'philosopher' for myself? Especially so when one looks at the list of the philosophers: Nietzsche, Hegel, Kant, Leibniz et al! How can I hope to place myself in the list? Am I the wise individual whom people call 'the philosopher'?

I look at this lovely word and see where it comes from. In the discourse of Socrates (or Plato), the philosopher is not the word for someone who is wise or who is a sage; far from it, the philosopher is the one who, lacking wisdom, longs for it (hence: philo-sophia: the lover/seeker of wisdom), as the lover erotically longs for his/her beloved. Far from possessing wisdom, and thus, far from being a wise person or a sage, he is rather the paradoxical figure of poverty and destitution: the richness of the philosopher, like the figure 'Eros' (who is impoverished and yet rich), lies in his/her irreducible destitution! What he does not have makes him rich!: A 'figure', truly understood, of humility (and abundance) and not a claim of possession! That is why in the Hellenistic intellectual world the philosopher is distinguished from the sage: the sage is much more than the philosopher.

Thus understood, I am indeed a philosopher—the destitute one!: Not someone who is wise, but the foolish fellow who, nevertheless, loves wisdom, and erotically longs for it. I am not a philosopher like those big names—Kant, Hegel, Leibniz—I am rather the little one, a little flower amidst tall trees, and I am happy to be just this little flower, because the sun shines on the tall trees as much as on this little flower! Somehow I have this crazy idea that the philosopher can, must, and should never a 'celebrity': there can't be 'philosophical festival' in the manner of 'a literary festival'; the novelist can hope to be a celebrity, an intellectual celebrity, but the philosopher must just be this little flower who turns her head wherever the sun shines in the sky.

After my death, or perhaps even before death, I shall one day be called a 'philosopher', or the little flower!

39. Attention, concentration

Never have I ever been so lucid in my life as nowadays, though I have never indeed been unclear or confused in fundamental concerns of my life. I like this lucidity about myself: there is a sense of freedom and opening that comes with it that is truly valuable, the lucidity and clarity as to what constitutes the substance of one's own existence, and what is its essential vocation and how to go about it. I now look into its depth, as if my gaze has become an ethereal light passing through a crystalline prism: my gaze intensely concentrated on the essential of life and not wavering, and thereby giving substance to my existence.

I needed this now more than ever before, though in fact I have never lacked this: the whole energy of my being concentrated on just one point, which being 'one', is nothing other than an abyss. It can be a paralysis of gaze, vertigo of thought, but it can also be precisely thereby the point from which radiates the infinite light of redemption.

40. Dignity and beauty

The beauty of a human being lies in the dignity that comes to him/her from the ethical-spiritual integrity of the whole person. This beauty has something of ineffable solitude and silence about it, so much so that every word that he utters is surrounded by a profound silence, and each time you are with him, even in the most intimate manner possible, he is still somehow inaccessible, solitary, and distant, a distance that shelters his beauty from the violence of our grasp.

The profoundest human being is also the most beautiful one. Closer to the divine than the base human being, his distance from our grasp at once calls us towards him, fascinating us with a beauty ever more new and ever more ancient, for dignity has this peculiar mode of its existence: while calling us to it constantly, it always seems to retreat to an ever more distance!

41. Aesthetics of existence

In my youth, much more than now, I used to have this inferiority complex: that I am not good looking enough! I like beautiful people, people who are blessed with beauty, and of course, beauty in all other forms and appearance. And I also admire—and this people may find a vanity in me—people who take care to appear beautiful, for I find this whole process of aesthetization and stylization, whether of appearance or of one's own existence, a tremendously beautiful work of the human race.

I like the wild beauty of nature, I wonder at its sublime beauty, but it moves me to see a beautiful landscape made by the human hand. When I see a dancer, I am fascinated: what and how a human being can create beauty by rhythmic movement of her body and face. This is why works of art have never ceased to fascinate me: how a human being can create beauty out of his voice, or with the help of colors on a canvas, or weaves a story of human suffering and joy in a beautiful novel form! And it is fascinating how in the hands of a sculptor the amorphous mass of rock disappears, and there appears a figure of a divinely beautiful goddess!

So when I realized that I am not blessed with physical beauty, I decided to accomplish beauty in other domains and in some other forms: I became attentive to my use of language so that I can hope to write beautiful prose. And I have discovered beauty in philosophy, for philosophy has come to mean for me—in which way I am a Platonist—a certain aesthetization, beautification and beatification of our inner existence! To philosophize means to beautify and beatify our existence. Even in our appearing to be beautiful in external forms there glows, dimly though, our infinite longing for an absolute beauty. I like certain perfection in a sentence structure written by a consummate writer; and I admire how the whole inner richness of our thinking is given a beautiful form by a thinker. And above all, I find this very word 'beauty' beautiful, and find the human language marvellous: could we have an understanding of what beautiful is if the word 'beauty' itself were not beautiful?

42. Infinite memory

There are some people whom one may have met just once, or a few times in life without ever closely interacting with them, and yet, for the rest of one's life one keeps them fondly in memory, and never ceasing to experience that profound, nameless inner affinity which one hardly feels in life with another human being, however intimately related the other may be. Thousands of people enter our lives and go, without leaving anything like a trace of an indelible memory, and it is paradoxical why some individuals with whom one hardly ever had any interaction, and yet they leave in us a memory so indelible and unforgettable! Against the dark sky of the past they stand like steadfast stars in our minds.

As one grows old, the future keeps shrinking for him and the past keeps growing bigger, and then, one starts looking back at the past more frequently than ever before. What, then, appear in front of our inner gaze, are those essential moments and essential relationships out of the innumerable myriad events of the past: the essential emerges, now purified in the fire of time, while the rest sinks into the night of oblivion. This is how we come to know what indeed are the essentials in one's life and what are not.

In my visit to the University of Tübingen a decade ago, I stayed in a philosopher's house for ten days and I have never met her after that. But that nameless love, distanced by a profound respect and nourished by a spiritual and intellectual kinship, has never disappeared from my memory. And some 20 years ago when I was a university student, I was taught by a professor for few months: even now, for more than half my life, I kept her in memory, and that nameless, profound love and respect I have had for her has remained undiminished all these days.

For someone at my age only the essential counts in life, someone who, for the sake of the essential, happily renounces the myriad inessential events of life to the night of oblivion. What we learn from experience, and not from books, is this: this distinction between the essential from the inessential, and to salvage, at least in memory—and then transform it in writing, if you are a writer—the essential from vanishing into the night of oblivion. The memory that redeems us is not of the past indifferential but the past that arrives to us purified, like gold, from the fire of time. It is not necessary how long you have lived with an event or an individual: you may have met him—a teacher, a student, a friend or a lover—just for a very brief period of time, but he stands still like eternity in time, while the rest sink into the vortex of fleeting time.

Living a life in the darkness of presence often does not give us proper perspectives. What one is undergoing at the present, which is tempestuous, and now affecting us wholly, may look stale after few years, and it too sinks like many other things into the abyss of the past. To grasp the essential of life in memory is not to be nostalgic: it is to look at life on a more comprehensive canvas, holistically, and without bias or prejudice. Events and individuals who happened to one's life, then, appear in a different light, now redeemed: one looks at the agony of one's past with a certain smile, forgiving the unforgivable, and accepting the inevitable. In the desolation of our existence, when life looks so empty, the redeemed past consoles us, and prepares us for the future that is still left of life.

43. Two kinds of sadness

There are two sorts of sadness: sadness because of the desolation of immediate existence, and the other, that truth infinitely exceeds one's grasp, and that only by abandoning all appropriation is the truth possible. In all abandonment there is sadness.

The more essential one's sadness is, the more spiritual and serene does it become. He who is thoroughly permeated by it is constantly kept in a certain 'reserve' or 'distance' in regard to the immediate form of worldly existence: a withdrawal from the truth of the world, but also an opening to the other truth where one stakes one's own existence.

44. Idea for one's life

He who does not live by an idea, and is not made solitary by having an idea is someone whose life is like vapour: he floats over everything and nothing, going in all directions like idle chatter or gossip, allows himself to be led by thousand distractions and evasions, and lives on them like parasites. He constantly needs someone around him, and if not anyone, at least something external to engage with—politics, virtual community, virtual pleasure, fantastic ideologies that never cease daily intoxicating us, and all the demands of the age. Such a person, when he grows old, becomes loquacious, prattling, peevish and cranky, petty and worldly wise, which means being mediocre and idiotic.

It is absolutely important for an individual to acquire an idea in one's life—one, singular and non-relative—to live every breath of one's life, and to sustain it, in absolute fidelity, throughout his whole life, and allow his life to be manifested through it, in all earnestness and in sobriety. Otherwise we become like a rudderless boat, floating without restraint hither and thither on the quotidian sea of banality, and at the mercy of every kind of weather.

I like this *askesis* of self-restraint: not to understand oneself in terms of the world (not to act like a worldly wise man), and not to give way to the demand of the age, as much as possible, only that which may help an individual to maintain bit of personal and intellectual integrity and inward depth. While we may meet hundreds of people every day—many of them will be far more superior to us in talent or in education, or in beauty and wealth—there will be hardly one in a thousand who has anything called 'idea'. Emptier in inwardness, more and more we will have the need to be diverted in the externals.

45. Solitude

The true idea of solitude is not that of lacking sociality, friends, or human company, but having an idea: more essentially someone has an idea, more solitary will he become. We can't approach him, however close we are to him otherwise (he is a friend, a colleague, or even a brother), still he remains somewhat, in an irreducible manner, distant. We can say that she is essentially in solitude who has an idea: the idea that individualizes her, singularizes her, and sets her apart in the very middle of our worldly existence.

46. I am a little flower!

For the rest of my life—the time that is left to me, however short or long—I am going to deal, philosophically and as philosopher, with the question of religion (for I am neither a mystic nor theologian).

Let this be clear to myself, and I have always been clear about myself: politics is not my vocation; I neither have the thickness nor enough faith in politics; it is not what I consider to be the highest vocation of human existence, and I can't put at stake everything of me into it; it soon wearies me out, every sort of politics and administration, petty or grand. I can't be too much into literature/literary studies, or art, or culture/culture studies: I get impatient too soon there, finding nothing much to be nourished on (I starved there!); I need something more austere, something that is suitable to my temperament, which philosophy for me is.

It is time; it has always been this time—of *Kairos*—to be decisive in one's life: one thing alone is necessary, and one must abandon oneself to it wholeheartedly. One can't change the world, however one likes to, for the world has its own law of becoming and an individual is nothing: what alone I can do, in a very modest and humble manner, to daily fulfil the little task—the little flower that I am!—that is given to me, to a perfection, and with my love and utmost attention. If I can fulfil this little task of my little, modest, individual life—which has its own infinity, for it is at once infinite—my life, at its end—which can occur at any time—will still make, so I hope, a lot of sense. Very quietly, calmly, in serene joy, in solitude, without aspiring for anything great, and without desiring to be a genius, I must keep working, early in the morning and late at night, to fulfil little by little what is given to me as my task, and to make sense of this little, fragile life of mine, with a lot of love for people around me and care for them without expecting anything in return, as much as possible for this selfish life.

Everything around me, in all its sickness, madness and futility has tormented me for sometime—oh, this immeasurable world-weariness!: this 'I can't go on...'—but I must not go on battling with this depression and despair anymore, but with faith, hope and love—these alone are the cure—keep doing little work little by little every day, that essential and unique work of my singular life: it is my singular destiny for which I am responsible alone, in absolute singularity! I must renounce 'the big' transformation (world-historical! national!, etc.) and concentrate on the little task of life: my philosophical studies, attending to people around me with understanding, love and care, and remain honest and authentic amidst mockery, irony and scepticism from the world. I cannot become a mystic and am not worthy to aspire for mystical union with God, but I still may be able to love him (that is enough!); I can't become a great philosopher, but philosophize nevertheless, in a little way, is still a possibility (that is enough!); I can't transform the world, but little transformation I can bring to myself, a little metamorphosis, a little joy and a little beauty (that is enough!).

Does the sun not shine—as St. Therese of Lisieux remarks—equally on the tall tree as much as on the most humble, unnoticed and un-cared, little flower?

I am that little flower!

47. Paradox of faith

When the order of the world is suffering shipwreck, and all around me debris and wreckages are piling up sky-high, and everywhere there is only anarchy and futility, the only thing is meaningful and worthy for me today is to cling all the more fervently, in utter fidelity, to the spiritual-intellectual task of my life, and to keep working on it steadfastly, patiently and in solitude, in humility and invisibility, having faith in God that a substantial part of it will be fulfilled.

To have this quiet faith in God in this 'human and all-too-human' world of monstrosity: this is the old-fashioned, inhospitable, incomprehensible and disagreeable paradox! And yet, lo!, the only thing that makes sense in this senseless world is that which is the extreme limit of sense: the paradox of faith!

48. Stranger to the World

In search of a nameless love—lo!—I have become homeless and a stranger to the world!

49. *Visio beata*

A vision, dim though, of a beauty more intimate and sweeter to me than I am to myself, and yet more remote than all the distance—is making me impatient and restless these days with an infinite longing.

The deeper a human being becomes through the inwardness of spirit, the more secret she has to bear. That one has to live another, an invisible and hidden life, denying all human communication apart from bare, most minimal hints, even from one's best friend and closest person: this is also a kind of suffering.

As if the vision of beauty has to inevitably traverse through the peril of suffering, this passing through the abyss of the night so that darkness may light up all the more dazzlingly...

50. To have one idea

To have one and only idea in one's life, and live or die for its sake, in utmost fidelity: it is this which gives a person his or her foundation of life. If something like that exists, then it does not really matter whether the world rewards you or not!

Most human beings live without any existential foundation. Like a rudderless boats we float hither and thither on the sea of the world, at the mercy of the unruly wind. What we need is to give existence its foundation—in an idea.

Each one of us, in our own way, is on a vast, unruly sea: the weather is incalculable and often demonic, the wind is often unpredictable, and the waves are immense and roaring all around us. I am on a little boat, fragile and precarious. Unless I have one absolute and fundamental idea—of existence—I will soon be shipwrecked! Thanks, it exists!

51. I am the vessel of transiency

Only in the complete surrender of the heart to God does human existence attain purity and serenity; outside God it is all suffering and pain...

Only through mortification of all egotism can we participate in the divine life where all is fire and yet does not annihilate us, for it is the fire of love that burns and dazzles us, and yet, does not destroy us by its violence. There we find true life where transiency passes away, as it is destined to pass away.

I am the vessel of transiency: my beloved gives me an eternal kiss on my ashen lips, and I become whole again.

52. Melody from my violin

To wrench a soulful melody out of the wounded strings of a violin: yea, that is the task.

53. To think with Heraclitus

At a certain stage of life when one comes to the shocking realisation of the inexorable and ineluctable flight of time, this cunning witch whom you cannot cheat, and that the invincible limit of all that exists which we call "death" is just here and now, very near, in its invisible presence, then he feels an urgency that is not like any other urgencies of life, for it defines what is "urgency" as such: the intensification of time as moment, not to be missed, when a phosphorescent appearing of life must be wrested from the invisible power of oblivion. One, then, hurries up, with no time to waste, with a messianic impatience: what exists far must come now at this moment and to this place, otherwise it will never come.

To live messianically is an intensity whose figure can be likened to a tightened bow: what is released, namely the arrow, is at once death and life. What brings death to us also gives us our life: I know no other definition of intensity than this. The other name of this intensity is "tragic".

Lectio divina

1. Comparing the incomparable

I must never compare my achievement, if there is any at all, with others (peers, friends, colleagues etc.), not even with myself, if only because the task of my life is infinite. For all comparison demands calculation, and "calculation is a finite category" (Kierkegaard). Only in relation to the infinite, in relation to which must I always fail, is the true comparison possible—which is no comparison—for here I must compare the incomparable. I must so measure my life that it must always exceed every measure ; in other words, the measure with which I have to measure my life, must be the immeasurable par excellence, for it is so very easy to measure with what is merely measurable. When this happens, and this may happen any time incalculably, my agony and despair—of having to fail—immediately turns into ecstasy and freedom, because it opens my existence, which is finite, to the infinitude that always exceeds and transcends it (which is the true meaning of ecstasy and freedom).

2. Existence and philosophy

It seems that books have not only their own life but also their own time of birth. Like a child who, if born pre-maturely, is born weak and, if born very prematurely is born dead. So books too must be given their own time for growth in the womb of our inner life. This is the reason why these days most of the books are so lifeless, mechanical and un-spirited; they are the aborted children of sterile intellects, born premature.

Today's academics are so impatient to publish—to fill their CVs, to get the next promotion, to be applauded by their colleagues and peers—that they neglect the very thing that is decisive and the essential *raison d'être* of all intellectual-spiritual creations: to enrich and transform the writer himself as much as the reader. For that very reason it is even more decisive that the inner life of the writer/scholar/philosopher himself be rich and profound; he must let his own existence enrich and nourish his creation and his creation to enrich and transfigure his existence in turn. Life and thought must interpenetrate each other in such a way that in the work of creation life itself pours itself like life-giving wine from the vineyard of creation.

3. *Lectio Divina*

In medieval Europe there existed a certain mode of reading called "lectio divina": reading as divination, a contemplative-meditative reading that understands a text as consisting of manifold layers of senses, one deeper than the other, disclosing itself as the reader acquires his spiritual eyes. So reading has, according to this idea, less to do with the cognitive appropriation of meanings but essentially is concerned with the existential transformation of the reader himself. As the reader grows deeper spiritually, the deeper senses of the text will be disclosed to him: the reader, thus, transforms the text as much as he is transformed existentially by the spiritual depth of the text.

With the development of modern historical-critical exegesis, concerned with the literal meaning (which is the only one of the fourfold of senses, according to the medieval conception of reading) of the text in sight of its cognitive appropriation—one that is suspicious of anything that has to do with the "spiritual"—so as exhibit political consequences. This kind of contemplative reading has almost completely disappeared. The retreat from cognitive violence with which "lectio divina" was concerned, has been replaced with the cognitive appropriation which is unique to modernity.

Nowadays contemplative reading is almost impossible. In today's world when we are bombarded with and constantly distracted by social media, social networking, advanced technological tools such as iPod, cell phones, emailing, digital humanities, etc—which has alarmingly decreased the attention span of the human race—contemplative reading is increasingly becoming rarer and rarer. While the reading habit of educated humans has increased to an unthinkable degree in today's world—people read too much these days: they read on flights, at bus stops, in canteens between breaks over a cup of coffee, in the midst of a crowd in the malls etc—any serious reading only a few people really practise.

If you take up a sermon by Meister Eckhart to read you will be amazed: he just takes a line from the Bible, spends his entire spiritual and intellectual energy on this one line with utmost concentration and intensity, and you will see how he builds a complete edifice of the spirit, so profound and beautiful, on the exposition of just this one line. Nearer to our own time, Kierkegaard in his upbuilding discourses practised something like this: he devotes 30 pages or more to the exposition of just one line from an apostle's saying, and it is so incomparably beautiful, ennobling, enriching and transforming. They don't seem to have the disease of the modern men—the anxiety to exhibit their learning, with endless footnotes and citations, with their "ontologies" and "epistemologies" (these two words are favourite of Indian academics).

Reading is for me like prayer. I must shut myself off from the world, not only intellectually but physically: hence my closed doors; I don't like to receive a phone call or receive a guest while I read. Many people don't understand this peculiar habit of mine ; they don't even understand the gravity, the seriousness, the earnestness of this act called " reading" ; for people what is important, urgent, grave is the daily work of everyday life, and they reduce every spheres of life to the management or bureaucratic dealings of everyday problems. The violence of this modern life—whether it is cognitive violence or the violence of administrative life—is incalculable; it is far more alarming than atom bombs, because it is invisible and mostly even imperceptible. Once you start to read a serious work, with great mood, someone calls you with the most urgent message—as if the earthquake is happening—that you must sign a paper: everything is lost at that moment, and you come back to that moment—sometimes not for the rest of the day—after long struggles and efforts. But this means nothing for the world (they are not even apologetic), while for me it has an enormous significance of life and death. Only recently I realised that this is the problem of the modern man as such: he does not know the importance of reading, the seriousness of contemplation, and the transforming effects of prayer; for him everything must be entertainment, including philosophy that can be read anywhere anytime. As prayer needs long preparation, both physical and mental—you have bathe, take off your shoes before entering the prayer room, wear something on your head, sometimes observe fast, and close your eyes and mind when you pray—so reading too needs preparation, a loving attention, a certain harmony of mind and body, a certain disposition. It cannot take place in all places, at all times, in all moods: we have to create it, make a place for it, and open our minds for it, clear a time for it.

For quite some time I have not been able do serious reading without being distracted and interrupted. As a result even if I read the whole day, I remain dissatisfied in the evening, like a long night of bad sleep full of nightmares. If I happen to read something, even for an hour, with certain concentration, I am happy. Our modernity is coming to us with a great price: we have forgotten to confront ourselves in solitude; solitude no longer exists; we constantly need diversions, distractions and entertainments. The result is a petty, narrow minded, narcissistic modern man: a disgusting sight.

4. Reading classics

More and more I am advancing in age, more and more my time machine is running backwards. I started my research for my doctorate on contemporary philosophical thought; then I moved back to focus on 19th century thought (culminating in my book on Schelling), and now I am going even more backward—to medieval thought, focusing on Meister Eckhart (while reading other thinkers of the epoch along with him—Augustine and Bernard).

When one reads, in the midst of the hustle and bustle of contemporary existence, a thinker from another epoch—far distant in time and place—one feels a vigour and a rejuvenation of spirit incomparable to anything that presently exists; more and more my hair is turning grey, more and more I am learning to prize the necessity of the vigour and renewal of the spirit. Reading Seneca, or Cicero, or even, for that matter, Montaigne, strangely ennobles us, and gives us the understanding that modern man is not necessarily the best of human beings that existed on this earth. Compared to Augustine, or a Plotinus, even the best of modern individuals from 20th century looks like a dwarf, a petty and self-seeking, narcissistic dwarf.

5. Growing old

We often see old people growing petty, cantankerous, suspicious or even infantile, and we often blame it on old age itself which is supposed to be the time for people to go senile. But I think this is not wholly correct.

The reason why some people grow petty in their old age is rather that they have in fact always been such, only that it is not manifested in such clarity. What was hidden in youth, in the subterranean depth of the buried life, has now come to manifestation, and we are appalled!

This is why we must so cultivate ourselves—in generosity, in magnanimity, in openness—that we grow old enriched, beautiful and wise. This cultivation and education is the task of a whole lifetime. It is necessary to be constantly engaged in intellectual and spiritual activity of some sort—daily reading, regular writing, daily prayer, deeper thinking and more generous understanding of life, by engaging in creative works of some sort that constantly elevate our soul—whether painting or music, dance or theatre.

Our intellectual-spiritual engagement with our life as a whole keeps our soul open, wide, deep, expanded; decades of arduous training is necessary even till the last moment of one's life. This is why some people in old age grow even more beautiful, which is reflected even in outer appearances. This patience with existence yields fruits that are of immense spiritual benefit.

We are so absorbed every day with the everyday demands of practical-worldly life—accumulating wealth, climbing the ladder of success, immersed in the daily affairs of politics—that we hardly give attention to the cultivation of the spirit, to the inward deepening of our life. So when we grow old—physically weak, no longer strong enough to battle with the world—that old pettiness, combined with deep insecurity and sense of vulnerability, comes to the full manifestation, and we grow more infantile than children.

6. The tragedy of an intellectual

For a solitary individual who pursues a fundamental intellectual vocation in a milieu which at best is a desert, a barren land, and who pursues it nevertheless without any external support, whether institutional or in the form of inspiration in a living community of friends who are spiritually akin to him, the biggest challenge is this: that he has to draw a prodigious amount of inspiration and enthusiasm—which alone makes possible a work of any value—from himself alone. However strong an individual is, and whatever prodigious amount of spiritual passion he bears, there comes every now and then a sense of exhaustion, the feeling of being emptied out—not of thought, or ideas, or even of language, but maintaining that sheer inspiration that is the condition of any work of value: 'how much', so the isolated individual tells himself, 'can I go on?' Then there are comes temptations in the desert: to give up the essential work of life, and to take refuge in the banality of quotidian existence that is satisfied with the petty fulfilment and enjoyments, a form of life lived for eating and sleeping, life which otherwise he has so far transcended. But now and here occurs the fall: degeneration has set in; he forgot his nobler existence, and has now got embroiled in the vicious circle of never-ending banality of chatter and politics. Now and then when he remembers his previous existence, he boasts with his friends of what he has achieved in life, in his golden youthful days, which he thinks is 'enough for a lifetime', and thus, in order not to confront the guilt that secretly and invisibly gnaws at his heart, he takes recourse to his past achievements and justifies the rest of his wasted life in its name. The only dream now he cherishes—since the rest is fulfilled: a beautiful wife/ handsome husband, children growing to be worldly successful just like him, a cosy house, preferably in a metropolitan city, and an insured income—is to write a memoir, something like an epitaph where he will leave behind the story of a unique existence—of worldly success, while forgetting his tragic fall that evokes from a young man pity and fear without *catharsis.*

7. With Derrida, *Sans papier*

Philosopher qua philosopher does not have a nation. The philosopher is someone who is without a passport: s/he may time-travel and space-travel everywhere anytime, *sans papier*, always in exodus!

8. Only the essential

Of the vast ocean of academic research in our contemporary world when knowledge has become a commodity just like anything else—perhaps a more prized commodity than anything else—most of the researches really are only banal at best, utterly lifeless, and most of the time carried on non-existent problems, while others have purely instrumental values which becomes outdated once they serve their purpose. For example, if you take any department of any university anywhere, suppose even the best university in India, you will see that most of the researches carried on there are really not-genuine, not at all of any serious value, just run of the mill or mediocre researches; they should best be called 'creative plagiarism' (as someone I forgot who coined this term), a kind of parasitic researches, researches carried on researches carried by other people who in turn carried their researches on some other scholars. With lot of luck you will find someone who is genuinely, existentially—pouring your entire existence into it—is genuinely doing something called 'research'. When one looks at this vast ocean of nonsense being carried out, and wreckage of nonsense piling upon wreckage, one can't but despair of being 'academic'. The sheer madness to be 'productive', like sophisticated machines, the hysteria and panic attacks that almost every one of us undergoes, the anxiety to cook up something that must sound new, and sheer noises that almost everyone makes around to exhibit, shamelessly, how much each one knows (each one is insanely prodigious and prodigal): this is a sheer pathological problem and seriously needs therapeutic treatments. Someone somewhere brings out a new 'theory', and becomes visible and being talked about, everyone rushes to know him and read him, as one hysterically shouts seeing someone from the entertainment industry on the stage.

Therefore it is good to take ' retreats' from this madness, and do something essential in solitude upon which one can dedicate, even sacrifice, one's entire life; to withdraw oneself from this great madness to work upon an idea—one and only one—for a whole lifetime and make one's life dependent on it. Only the essential matters in life, even if it is just one thing, and the essential is always just one thing: in a fundamental sense, for a genuine scholar or a philosopher, there can only be one research project and only one philosophical question; only for mediocre scholars there are hundred questions and hundred answers. Only one thing is needful: this is the purity I must now pursue with uncompromising rigor and patience. Ultimately this is what will ultimately matter. I don't have to have that hysteria, panic attack or madness for that.

9. Simplicity of philosophy

There is a simplicity which is an entirely different thing from 'simplifying'. When people complain that philosophy, admirable and lofty though it may be, is too difficult (not simple) and abstract (if they don't like philosophy they will call it "full of jargon")a subject, and ask me to make it simple for them ("tell me what 'this' means") , they confuse here 'simplicity' and ' simplifying'. The fact is that philosophy, which deals with the highest thing(s) of existence, is precisely the most simple, for what the highest and most noble is, is also the most simple; and yet, precisely for that matter, it can't simply be simplified: it is not automatically available to our immediate and natural cognition, and to our immediate, natural, sensuous mode of being. What the most simple is, because it is the highest and most noble, needs extreme spiritual and intellectual efforts and *askesis* from us; only through rigorous and systematic, even austere and hermetic exercises we can attain that simplicity. What actually many people want me to do is not to make philosophy simple for them but to simplify philosophy for them, but philosophy can't be simply simplified: when one does that, it takes away from philosophy, its nakedness, it's pure encounter with truth.

Frankly speaking, most people are intellectually lazy; they want everything immediately available, like commodities in today's world of mass consumption for instant gratification where everything has to be immediate and transparent to our cognition and appropriation; in other words, our "instrumental rationality" can't tolerate anything that resists immediate appropriation and possession. Because philosophy has to do with radical dispropriation and dispossession, philosophy is the most useless mode of thinking and being in today's world. On the other hand, every academic wants to sound lofty and sophisticated; so they put the decorative cream of philosophy on top of the main dessert, for which they need philosophy, desperately, and only a 'simplified' philosophy please!

Therefore, I actively discourage people from philosophy and say that it is difficult. But here it is only the half truth that I say.

Philosophy is rather simple; nothing is so purely simple and simply so pure than philosophy and theology; but, for today's violent academics of "instrumental rationality", this simplicity is extremely difficult; it is, in other words, a difficult simplicity.

10. Sober prose

I would like to create for myself, and am trying to do so, such a sober prose of extreme concentration and attention where not a single word or even a punctuation mark is dispensable: each word must be pregnant with senses and is suffused like a tightened bow. My method is that of a sculptor: a great deal elimination of the gross matter only to retain the elements where "even the stones too cry out". Henceforth, all my books will be much smaller in size.

11. The art of reading

Lot of our intellectual growth depends not only on what we read but how we read. Therefore we must attend not only to what we read but also to how we read. While the former appears to be more or less obvious, but the latter is hardly obvious to us. We not only read what we read indiscriminately, we also read how we read indiscriminately. It is far more difficult, and far more challenging to read 'well' in today's digital world of knowledge than ever before: what to read when so much is available? Here the question of how to read can't even be posed, unless we know what to read.

The medieval religious thinkers had the conception of the four-fold sense of a text. In today's scholarly world which is dominated by one kind of reading—that of 'critical-historical'—the old concept has withered away and is displaced. The inner life of a work which animates the inner unfolding of its movement must be discovered and be made manifest: it calls for an inner eye for divination and discernment that can only be cultivated for long years, and needs infinite patience with loving labour. Which course in which

University trains young students and researchers in how to read? It is difficult to pose this question to today's young generation of knowledge hungry academics: nobody has patience, and nobody has time to choose what to read; everyone is hurrying up, reading indiscriminately, going from one book to the other, as if one is on a marathon race of reading, eager to complete one book after another like a famished person devouring food without chewing! As a result, despite a prodigious number of books that every one of us reads, there is no adequate intellectual-spiritual growth and enrichment: they just make us lethargic, vain, arrogant, and at least intolerably boring.

In my student days I used to read like a famished man, devouring, or someone who is on a marathon race. I have now completely transformed my method of reading: I spend more time deciding what book to pick up and when, and I read fewer hours than ever before. I read slowly and patiently, giving lot of my time, and doing what I call 'contemplative reading'. To read now needs more mental preparation for me, as if I am going to a temple. Then I decide the hours which book to read where (office, in coffee shop, at home) and when (morning, afternoon, at night); I don't read any book anywhere. The whole task and purpose of reading is no longer to know what there is in the book, what knowledge or information it will give me, etc. but: what transformation or enrichment it will have for me, and how it will help me deepen of my inwardness. I have become rigorous, very methodical, a systematic kind of reader, and it is really helpful that way. It does not really matter how many books you read, and to be encyclopaedic, it is more important which book you pick up and how, in a certain manner, you are reading, entering into the inner movement of the thinking universe that the book opens for you.

12. The world of silence

The modern individual does not know how to speak; s/he only prattles. To speak it is essential that one listens, or learns to listen. In all listening—so that listening to be possible—there must be silence around it, and we must give it time so that what we have to listen may come to us, arrive to us. Therefore, to listen is always, first of all, listening to silence: only those who listen to silence may listen at all. To listen to silence is, thus, not one kind of listening among others; it is listening par excellence: it is listening to listening.

The modern individual does not have time—to listen, and consequently s/he knows not silence. Therefore s/he prattles away time. To speak is to have time: time and speech come from the same origin—from the inner depth of a great silence and solitude. In every essential speech there resound the voices of the origin, the voices of silence. One who listens to silence listens to the essential language which resounds in the voices of the wind, in the murmur of the waves, in the rustling of leaves, and in the humming of the sea. The human speech is surrounded by the vast silence of being and nothing, so that in every essential human word it repeats, echoes, resounds! One who speaks the essential creative word must give at the same time voice to the silence that inaudibly resounds in every utterance without which there is neither voice nor speech. This great silence is not a mere privation of speech; it is what gives speech its temporality to arrive so that when it arrives, it always sounds as if for the first time. In all essential word creation renews itself.

13. Listening

I am marking a profound transformation taking place in my thinking these days: while I used to think and write in a certain argumentative manner (which is required of a scholar or a philosopher in this academic place), though in a manner that is very different from what we generally call 'argumentation' (I call it 'critical thinking'), my thinking is now becoming increasingly meditative in nature. This has some real importance for me: I am no longer keen on polemics—or, keen on polemics only secondarily—whether in private discussions or in public stage; a certain reserve, or restrain—not to play all one's cards at once—is growing silently within me, making everything about me slow and patient: thinking comes in slow pace, and a great deal of time I spend in solitude to listen to what is coming to me, for what is essential comes often in silence, imperceptibly, "in dove's feet" (Nietzsche). So I have to be in utmost attention, waiting in time's patience, for what is to disclose itself to me. As it were, thinking is to be a prayer that demands, and that effects in turn, a certain inner transformation of being: it is this, the profound 'experience' of thinking, that is now of real importance to me than anything else.

The modern individual is too eager to speak, and is too talkative a person, and no doubt, hardly anyone listens: the sound of the drop of a dew on flower, the muffled cries of the other (hu)man, the melancholy wind of the deserts...in other words, the modern individual does not, or better, shies away from the 'experience' of the unspeakable and the unnameable which is the origin of speech, and which can only come to us, in all plenitude and fecundity, first of all in listening: in listening not only to nature, but even the human and the divine disclose themselves to us. The modern condition is a flight from divinity and nature; it makes everything a mere servile instrument of domination and calculation, of which technology is the best example. The modern human being does not know what 'humanity' means: that it is the silent reserve of the unspeakable which, precisely thereby—and this is the paradox—is open to speech that addresses, or rather responds to the call from nature and from divinity. As a light to illumine needs some darkness around it, or some other light against darkness, so humanity to know what it is, needs what is other than the human—the other finite beings, and the infinite above it. This is why humanity needs nature and divinity: this need, this destitution, this fragility—that modern human civilization wants to get rid of—is the precise source of human fecundity and plenitude, of his inexhaustible resource and infinite responsibility.

14. The gift of being

The modern individual is never free from and for himself. Look at him in the vacations he takes once after months or weeks of toil:

he is still thinking of his work, calculating his profits and losses, worried about his rivals and anxious about his immediate future; he works on his laptop on his flights, receives business calls after a lovely spa experience in luxury hotels, constantly instructs his subordinates about what they should do in his absence. Look at him when he goes to the temple; he is still thinking only about himself: praying to God to grant him some worldly success, as if God exists only for the purpose of granting his silly and petty profits and gains (what an ignoble God he would then be! I don't like such a God!). He is never truly free for anyone—for other human beings, for God and above all, for himself! He encounters nobody anywhere: the beauty of nature passes him unnoticed (he is still taking 'selfies' even on a lovely mountain top!); the pure joy from the divine remains unknowable to him (since God only exists to guarantee his worldly success); the joy of being with other human beings does not exist for him (every human relationship is for him only for mutual benefits). How wretched and miserable to be constantly embroiled only in one's immediate worldly concerns and only in one's own concern, and never for a moment to be free from himself and for himself.

Most often the source of our misery and wretchedness is ourselves: we don't learn to accept ourselves ('oh I want to slim down'! 'Oh I have done nothing in life'! 'Oh all my friends are getting married and my marriage is nowhere in sight!; etc. etc.), and we hardly ever learn to accept this gift of existence, out of which comes so many imaginary anxieties and so many worries about non-existing things ('Oh my husband must be going with someone'; 'Oh she has got a job and I will never have anything'!): all these things make us constantly only concerned about ourselves, making us selfish and petty.

The only way to be free for oneself is by giving oneself a vocation of life which can nourish and sustain one's life, through which life opens itself to infinitude, and releases the innumerable demands of immediate life for infinity, a vocation for the sake of which one can happily give up one's petty self: only an infinite can do this.

15. My small library

One thing I am really happy about is my small private library: a small library of a few thousand books, I have collected—with a lot of thinking and discernment—some of the greatest books of all time, basically of philosophy, theology and mystical writings. The idea is not only to carry out some fundamental research work which I have been able to project, but also to sustain my spirit and intellect for a lifetime. Thus I collect those books to nourish the deepest and sustained needs of my spirit.

Over the years I have learnt to evolve a methodology of collecting books: a rigorous method, which I meticulously apply, in the way that I have made a certain method of reading and writing which I would like to apply in letter and spirit. I don't, and I no longer, read, write and collect/buy books mindlessly and haphazardly.

Life is incredibly short, especially when one thinks of the infinite task of one's life, and of the infinite treasure island of spirit that one is to explore. This acute consciousness of mine about the brevity of human life, of my own life, and this understanding that a mere life—a bare physical and immediate, sensuous, biological life—is not worth much, and that spirit and intellect alone have something redeeming about life, it is this consciousness and understanding that has about it something of Socratic demon: like an infinitely vigilant lantern, it guides me early in the morning and later in the evening, and thereby, lending my inner life a certain intensity, a certain light and beauty, and also a certain sense of truth and meaning.

I can't say that I have learnt how to live, or how to die, but it is a question—and old, or rather an ancient question—which I think worthy to be asked by anyone, wherever one, is and whatever one, is. The highest and the most profound questions of human life are also the basic and the most simple question: what we need is just openness, a certain longing and achievement of freedom for oneself and from oneself, a readiness to recognize and to give up what we generally cling to, and which also happen to be nothing of essential and decisive interest in life.

So I am collecting books that can only have a certain existential meaning, of transformation and inward deepening—for me: and this is my only method, and it is, believe me, working quite well.

16. Philosophy

What I love about philosophy, among so many things, is its austerity and serenity: the philosopher knows, as much as the poet and the artist, ecstasy and agony of inspiration (or, the lack of it) but it is not possibly the decisive thing about philosophy. What is decisive is the fire of mortification that phenomena (or, experience) undergo to arrive at the sober prose of ideas which in turn transfigures and redeems them. It is this asceticism—*askesis*—which gives the phenomena a new glow in the sober gleam of serene blessedness, as if sanctifying them, and thereby anticipating the beatitude: it is this *askesis* which is peculiar to philosophy , in a much qualitatively different sense, that makes me love philosophy. I always love the sobriety that lies in the measure with which, when deepened by the 'dazzling darkness' (Pseudo-Dionysus) of the night, the fire of mortification burns on the landscape of the immeasurable!

17. The double vision of the philosopher

The philosopher should at once maintain unconditional fidelity to the absolute and yet an ironic distance from the immediate mode of being: this double vision, at once creative and critical, lends depth to the philosophical vision and makes it receptive to the manifestation of truth.

18. The generosity of St. Augustine

When one takes up a St. Augustine, or someone like him, it is like I have been so long in a closed room where the air has grown stale and now suddenly I am exposed to the sea, the vast and open sea with its mysterious waves rising from eternal depths, and winds blowing from nameless sources, while my gaze opens to the blue sky above: expansive, lofty, infinite. It is as if one has been sick for long and suddenly one feels health and vigour again.

19. The silent cry

Today everyone shouts, hardly anyone thinks. The language of thinking is not a shout, but a silent cry that pierces the violence of the shout and shatters it altogether.

20. The night of silence

At the depth of each word that we utter there lies a prodigious night of silence. If this silence is the origin of language, the word is the opening up of time: it is here love happens between mortals, between the mortal and the divine, between the human and the world. It is here the battle for justice is to be fought and to be won.

21. Consolation of philosophy

What I most prize about philosophy these days is the distance—and even certain detachment—that it gives me in regard to the immediate mode of existence (whether my own particular immediate existence or the immediate social world): from the heart of the clamouring world, the world that is shrieking and groaning, it opens up for a time of silence and a space of serenity, and gives me the measure, exceeding all available measures, in relation to which existence is to be understood, lived and undergone, without having to sink into the incessant whirlpool of worldly reality. A stability in the midst of the vortex of worldly existence, firm and yet loving, patient with an infinite patience with the earthly life, to dwell in the midst of the world, and yet dwell like an eternally wandering pilgrim with an infinite renunciation and abandonment: what is more prize worthy, and a better consolation than this in these desolate days?

Agony and Ecstasy of Love

1. Law and love

Two questions now occupy me—law (and religion), and love (in religion/mysticism)—demanding that I carry on two researches at the same time (since I would not like to abandon or postpone any of these "delicious" questions): fascinating material is now in my hand—some of these documents are precious jewels of human history—opening me simultaneously to two infinite 'realms of gold'(Keats), and yet, on the other hand, threatening to engulf me in the abyss of their beauty and light. The last two years are absolutely important to me, as will be important the coming years: years of exploration and discovery, and this opening to new dimensions of truth.

Apart from our talent and intelligence, and our ability to do hard work and systematic-rigorous working style, what is important—and I consider this absolutely important—is keeping our soul pure and open to infinity that is possible in our finite life. With mere talent and hard work, one of course can produce many books and can have long CVs, but they will be abortive-mechanical products of sterile intellects, with no spirit and breath of life animating within it; none really is benefited and is transformed by these mechanical products. It is difficult to convey this: in the purity of our soul which is open, there happens or occurs a truth and a beauty; and when that happens, it becomes imperative for a thinker or a poet or a mystic to give that absolute event a language, a song, a color on a canvas. It is out of this great invisible wellspring of our inner existence that the great spiritual works of humanity have emerged. This mystery of the origin is unspeakable and incommunicable, and yet, this is the very origin of all speech and communication. Only by mortification or renunciation of our egotism this purity can be affirmed in the depth of our being—in love.

I want to understand this secret of love that is more primordial than the law, the enigma of the "law" of this love which is without law (of force, of sovereignty, of power): something within tells me that here lies the fulfilment of human existence, its "beatitude". I now need a language of "concepts" or "names"—since neither do I make music nor do I paint—to translate this.

2. Love and knowledge

All genuine knowledge begins in love and ends with love. Love and knowledge are, therefore, not opposites. Love is the origin of knowledge, and its fulfilment.

To participate in this fullness of life, in the overflowing and outpouring of love, one must begin by works of mortification—of our egoism and worldly economics. Love conjoins our life with death, where death is no longer objection to life but, as works, a passage to begin a new life.

Knowledge without love is worth nothing: it is only a trick of charlatans, a sleight-of-hand by tricksters. Only love breathes life and its beauty in knowledge to transfigure our mortal existence, and thus renews the divine image in which we are created. In this image we love all creatures: an infinite compassion without condition that alone is beatific and redemptive.

To contemplate this beatitude and redemption, in knowledge—beginning in love and ending in love—is the highest task of the philosopher.

3. 'Love never dies'

Some years ago someone told me: 'love never dies'. It sounded like sentimental truism, as if she does not know the other side of love: that love is so intimately connected with death and work.

Now I see that she was right: more than death, it is by eternity—an eternity of a sort—that love is intimated, and it is this which is the enigma, the mystery, the secret of what love is all about.

It is this enigma of love that I am concerned with: seeing it with the philosophical gaze of inwardness, without the violence of cognition, a gaze that lovingly allows itself to undergo the process of "crystallization" and makes manifest the truth against the sky of oblivion.

4. Love's immortality

I increasingly cherish the idea—in my imagination—of a love which does not have to be tied down to sexuality, a love more or less independent of sexuality, a love independent of any names/attributes that the institutions of the world give to it; it is love, if it were to exist, that is not weighed down by the demands of place (that we have to live together, or even have to see each other), a love that flourishes even in the distance of seven seas, without having to meet the other; the possibility of intellectual love, or a love spiritual, if such a love is possible, where spirits engage across the seas of solitude, or even loneliness, in a profound conversation that exceeds even the measure of life, and can even struggle with the death, with this cunning old witch called "time".

5. Woman in love

In many ways I am like a woman in love: what she says in just one glance, an eloquent poet cannot say in a thousand words.

6. Midnight thoughts: of good, evil and other things

In all her actions and thoughts the human being, knowingly or not, seeks beauty. The possibility of absolute annihilation of this vision of beauty is what defines the radical evil. Since this is mere possibility, and always a possibility, evil becomes more and more malicious, like unconsummated consuming fire that seems to devour more it is dissatisfied in its hunger: in this impotency of evil precisely—and this is the paradox of evil—lies the potentiality of its destructiveness. The horrors of the last one hundred years are only empirical examples of this evil out of its metaphysical abyss.

We must think of Good which is not equal, but more originary than radical evil, the Good that infinitely surpasses the possibility of evil: love alone, in its infinite vision of beauty, exceeds the horrors of evil. The abyss of love is not the fire that annihilates without atonement; it is the fire that gives warmth and light to the life of the spirit that passes through all annihilation and maintains itself in it, only waiting to be redeemed from the violence of evil.

To contemplate this good and beauty surpassingly glorious, without the violence of cognition, is the beatific vocation of the philosopher and the poet. His *vocation* is to invoke or to call, through *voce* (meaning voice that is living), beauty to come: this is why in Greek the word for beauty (*kalon*) is a cognate word for calling or *invocation* (*kaloun*), as Plato discusses in his dialogue called *Cratylus*.

7. Life as life

The mere life—the mode of being as this immediate and sensuous life—makes me recoil from its sight in despair or in anguish and sometimes even in disgust, like the one who despairs when he sees an animal annihilated by a tiger or lion, and he sees the nothingness of mere life exposed open in all laceration and abjection. This is why intellectual and spiritual creations—this whole work of art, philosophy and religion—have never been for me mere garbs over the sensuous and immediate mode of life, creations that are not mere instrumental means to achieve something; they are the very possibility of life, *life as life*, through which I can come to terms with and redeem the 'annihilation-character' of mere life. This is the source of the irreducible melancholy that veils all life, more so of human life. It is the poet, the philosopher and the mystic (science knows nothing of this!) who has to be the melancholic being, not so as to be submerged and buried into the underground of death, but to redeem it through works of truth and beauty.

8. Ecstasy of love

The end of knowledge is in itself not knowledge but an ecstasy of love. Knowledge is the process of mortification through which all that is dross is purified and abandoned so that infinity may present itself to us in its purity. This process of mortification is suffering: this is why it is said that knowledge is suffering.

9. Love and justice

Love and justice, in two different ways, exceed the violence of judgment. This is why judgment tends to be wordless and wants to deny its opening in language. Love and justice are, thus, the linguistic events par excellence. By opening up the space of time, the word summons up love on our lips, so that each time our lips part and open there may outpour the wine of love.

10. Nameless good

To know that in the encounter with the nameless Good all knowledge becomes nothing: what kind of knowledge is this? Neither knowledge of particular things nor a particular knowledge of things, it approaches towards that which cannot be seen with naked eyes, so much naked do we have to be, so that to see really would mean to see nothing at all, that is, to see nothing, to see nothing else, to see everything as nothing.

There is in our innermost being a deep, profound silence: time stops there, for we have nowhere to go, and we don't come to it either; so it happens without our having to come and having to go!: An event without time where nothing "happens": a happening without anything to happen.

I don't understand myself there any more, I don't have anything " in" myself to know in myself, while I understand everything in it where nothing "be".

11. Vanishing of love

It appears that love is vanishing today more than ever before. While the extreme form of mass consumption of today's world of neo-liberalism has indeed liberated—in the manifest, but not the only, sense—our sexuality from various traditional repressions, the nearly complete and totalised sexualisation of all aspects of our existence has made each of us purely self-seeking, narcissistic individuals, a narcissism daily fed with phantasms by spectacles: it is the phantasm of the instant gratification of senses and of a plenitude of a pleasure so overflowing as to be inhuman. We demand from our bodies too much, too much we overtax our organs in pursuit of a plenitude that never exists to that degree, and we determine our human relationships too much on the basis of these phantasmal possibilities. The other (person) appears to us at once just as a source of our plenitude, and yet, on the other hand, nothing more than an abject, impoverished object, purely existing for one's plenitude which masks, in unforeseen ways, nothing less than the laceration of our consciousness.

This devouring and malicious hunger for self-fulfilment that consumes us in a never-ending fire: this torment is the peculiar gift of today's specular and spectacular world of mass consumption. With this there is the disappearance of love, our inability to see the other human more than an object of our self-satisfaction, and our inability to form a human communion on the basis of the profound movement of the heart towards the other without the economy of profit!

12. Sentences without verbs

To really know what one has to do with life, and to do it with unconditional fidelity and severe earnestness: this gives life its intensity, depth and necessary orientation...

To live without it is like writing sentences where you find a plethora of adjectives, conjunctions and endless interjections but without a verb. Most of our lives most often are such sentences where verbs don't exist...